When you LOVE a MAN Who Loves HIMSELF...

When you LOVE a MAN Who Loves HIMSELF...

SOURCEBOOKS CASABLANCA™
AN IMPRINT OF SOURCEBOOKS, INC.®
NAPERVILLE, ILLINOIS

w. keith campbell, PhD

Published by Sourcebooks, Inc.
P.O. Box 4410, Naperville, Illinois 60567-4410
(630) 961-3900
FAX: (630) 961-2168
www.sourcebooks.com

Campbell, W. Keith.
  When you love a man who loves himself / W. Keith Campbell.
    p. cm.
  Includes bibliographical references.
  ISBN 1-4022-0342-X (alk. paper)
  1. Narcissism. 2. Man-woman relationships. I. Title.

BF575.N35C36 2005
646.7'7--dc22

Printed and bound in Canada
TR   10   9   8   7   6   5   4   3   2   1

For Stacy and McKinley Grace

Acknowledgments

The ideas presented in the book are the result of research collaboration with many terrific colleagues. Although there are too many to list all of them, my thanks to: Dr. Roy Baumeister, Angelica Bonacci, Dr. Brad Bushman, Amy Brunell, Dr. Andy Elliot, Dr. Julie Exline, Dr. Eli Finkel, Dr. Craig Foster, Josh Foster, Dr. Adam Goodie, Dr. Madoka Kumashiro, Dr. Glenn Reeder, Dr. Eric Rudich, Dr. Caryl Rusbult, Dr. Constantine Sedikides, Dr. Jeremy Shelton, Ilan Shrira, Dr. Jean Twenge, and Dr. Kathleen Vohs. I am also grateful to Marrianne Bellino, Amy Brunell, Kathleen DiPaolo, Drs. Jeff and Jodie Green, Bill McMahan, Lisa Reichenbach, Pam Riddle, Deb Werksman, and, in particular, Linda Konner, for reading drafts of this manuscript and supplying detailed feedback and suggestions. Finally, I would like to thank all the research participants who were in our studies and all the individuals who were willing to share their stories.

Table of Contents

Introduction ix

Chapter 1: Who is a Narcissist?. 1

What is Narcissism? 1

Damn, I'm Good (But I'm No Mother Teresa)—
Understanding the Difference Between Narcissism
and High Self-Esteem 11

Entitlement—Narcissists' Secret Ingredient 17

Mr. Fun 23

Do Not Look at the Man Behind the Curtain
(or, Maintaining the Narcissist's Illusion). 28

When the Bubble Bursts (or, What Happens When
the Truth Breaks Through). 33

Six Other Questions about Narcissists 39

Chapter 2: Narcissists in Relationships 49

Being the Top Dog (or, It's All About Winning) 50

I'm in Control Here. 58

Empathy? Caring? Huh?. 62

Can We Talk about Me for a Moment? 67

Wandering Eyes (or, What You Don't Know Won't Hurt You). . 71

Commitment is Great—for Other People (or, "The List") . . . 77

What do Narcissists Call Love? 85

Bling, Bling: Narcissism and Materialism 91

Manipulative Weasels—Emotion and Deception 100

Changing Places, Changing Faces. 104

Chapter 3: Why Get Involved with a Narcissist?. 111

   Making a Big Entrance. 111

   The Old Bait and Switch. 118

   The Illusion that Other People are Like You 123

   Narcissists Try Harder (or, The Myth That

   All Good Men Are Taken) 130

   Addicted to Drama and Excitement 136

   The Great Satisfaction Drop. 142

   The Double Curse of Dating Narcissists. 153

Chapter 4: What Can You Do About It?. 161

   Don't Do It—It's a Trap! 161

   Have I Done It? Analyzing Your Relationship 169

   Okay, I've Done It—Can Narcissists Change? 179

   So, Should I Stay or Should I Go?. 188

Chapter 5: Why Do I Always Date Narcissists?. 199

   Is It Society's Fault? 200

   Is It the Narcissist's Fault?. 205

   Is It My Fault? 212

   Never Dating a Narcissist Again 215

Research Notes 227

Introduction

Before I begin to lecture in my romantic relationships class, I usually ask if anybody has anything interesting to talk about. A few weeks ago, a student raised her hand and said that she had been at the spring fraternity formal with her boyfriend. At the formal, they announced several awards, one of which was the award for the "most hook-ups during spring break." Her boyfriend, it turned out, was the winner.

At this, the whole class quieted down. I asked what her boyfriend did after the announcement. She went on to say that he went to the podium to make a brief acceptance speech, which went something like, "What can I say? A lot of alcohol and a lot of girls." (Truly a modest person!) He then walked off the podium and stood next to her again.

She, of course, was somewhat shocked and upset. They had been dating for over a year and she knew nothing about this. He turned to her and asked why she was upset. (Not only a modest person, but caring too!) She replied that it might have something to do with his infidelity.

At this point, I had a pretty good idea that we were dealing with a relationship with a narcissist, so I asked, "He said it was your fault, right?"

She laughed a bit and said that he had gotten angry and blamed her for "ruining his formal." He also said that the infidelities didn't mean anything, and that he hadn't told her because he didn't want her to get upset (more deep concern on his part, of course!).

Someone in the class asked what she did, and she said that she ended things with him right there. The students in class were impressed at how tough she was. I asked her a few more questions about her relationship. As I had expected, the now ex-boyfriend turned out to have been charming, attractive, outgoing, and extroverted. He was also a bit cocky. And, of course, he had been lying to her about his commitment for a long time. In short, he sounded like a typical narcissist. I explained to her that her story was unfortunately pretty familiar, and that I would spend a full week lecturing on narcissism later in the semester. I went back to setting up the day's lecture, and several of the students commiserated with her and quickly told her that they had had similar experiences.

I have been studying narcissistic men for the last decade. These are men that have very positive opinions about themselves. For example, a man thinks that he is highly attractive and intelligent. At the same time, he also has relatively negative opinions of most others. In fact, instead of looking for emotionally close relationships, he uses other people to maintain his own self-love. He derogates the success of others. He competes with and dominates others. In the instances where he can't beat 'em, he joins them. For example, this man will associate with popular or successful people in order to keep up his own self-love. In psychological literature, we call these individuals *narcissists* because they are seen as similar to the mythical Greek figure "Narcissus", who fell in love with his own reflection.

My reasons for studying narcissists have been purely academic. I have been fascinated by the way that individuals with inflated and unrealistic self-views navigate their way through social life. How can someone who is basically average go through life thinking that he is a "ten"? How does someone who is no more successful than many other people actually think he is king of the universe? How does someone change his social world to fit his inflated self-image? Somewhat on a whim, I began studying how narcissists experience romantic relationships. This research resulted in a doctoral dissertation on narcissism and romantic attraction. This topic has continually proven to be very exciting because, frankly, seemingly normal and well-adjusted people do all sorts of strange things in their romantic relationships.

While I was engaged in my academic research on the subject of narcissism, I noticed a strange occurrence. Every time I talked about narcissists' romantic relationships in the classroom—or even with friends—women would seem to pay particular attention to what I was saying. The women would at first get a puzzled look in their eyes, then start nodding, and finally have an "a-ha" experience. Then the responses would come: "You know, I dated a guy like that once...what a jerk." "My roommate is dating a guy like that, he keeps cheating on her and she keeps letting him." "Why did I go out with a guy like that?" "Can you change someone like that?" Often the individual had never really put the pieces together. She knew that there was something wrong with the relationship, but learning about narcissism allowed her to see the full picture.

I more recently had this experience confirmed with a much larger sample of people. One of our recent academic studies was mentioned in the popular press. It started out as a very brief article on the Yahoo website, then an article appeared in the *New York Post*, followed quickly by an article in the *Atlanta-Journal Constitution*. The next thing I knew, the research was mentioned in a host of brief newspaper and magazine articles and I was bombarded with emails from across the globe asking about narcissism in relationships. I was amazed.

This overwhelming response was really surprising to me for several reasons. First, I am not used to people (other than fellow psychologists) actually being interested in my academic research. Usually when an academic starts talking, people's eyes glaze over! Second, men do not appear to find narcissism to be a big romantic problem. Certainly men have dated narcissistic women (indeed, narcissistic women act in ways that are very similar to narcissistic men), but this does not seem to affect men as much. Finally, I did not know how pervasive the experience of dating narcissistic men actually was. The majority of the women I have spoken to seem to have had this experience.

My goal in this book is to describe what it means to "love a man who loves himself." This is an experience that is shared by far too many women and can have a negative impact on their lives. My hope is that the realizations I have witnessed, in my students and from those who have emailed me, can translate to a wider audience.

Most of the ideas presented in this work are the result of academic research conducted by a host of excellent academic psychologists, my collaborators, and myself. I have also added my more speculative insights, as well as the insights of practitioners in the fields of clinical psychology and psychiatry. Finally, I have included many stories and examples that have been told to me. In most cases the stories have been modified to maintain the privacy of those involved. The book is not meant to be at all "academic." It is written for people who have never taken a psychology course. For those interested in gaining a deeper education on the topic of narcissism, I have included a list of academic references at the end, along with more detailed discussions of theoretical issues.

Chapter One

Who is a Narcissist?

What is Narcissism?

Arrogant, cocky, self-centered, selfish, self-absorbed, egotistical, egomaniacal, full of himself, God's gift to the universe, player, play-boy, conceited—all of these terms have been used to describe a certain type of man. In fits of anger, they are often strung together, as in: that arrogant-self-centered-conceited-egotistical-jerk. There is something about this type of man that brings out the fury in women and can be extremely damaging to them as well, especially in romantic relationships. Here is the basic story.

> Step 1: You meet a man who is self-confident, perhaps a little cocky, and physically attractive.
> Step 2: He presents himself as successful, popular, and important.
> Step 3: He is somewhat smooth or charming.

Step 4: You feel an immediate sense of attraction—he may be the one!

Step 5: You start a relationship.

Step 6: For a brief time you are very excited—you may even feel special or important.

Step 7: He becomes controlling and manipulative.

Step 8: He cheats on you.

Step 9: He still does enough positive things to keep you confused.

Step 10: You eventually realize that he might not be the guy who he said he was.

Step 11: The relationship (finally!) ends.

Step 12: You keep thinking about this person: how could this person you cared for be so nasty?

Step 13: Your friends repeatedly assure you that he was no good, but it is still difficult to let go.

Now, compare this to the standard story about dating a decent guy:

Step 1: You meet a man who is genuinely nice and sincere.

Step 2: You go out a few times and get to know each other.

Step 3: You find that the more you know him, the more attracted you become.

Step 4: You get involved in a relationship where there is caring and emotional intimacy.

Step 5: The relationship might end (most relationships do) because of various circumstances.

Step 6: You do not feel confused about the relationship
and may even remain friends with the man.

These episodes, of course, do not always happen exactly this way; sometimes various elements are different or missing and sometimes things are more complex. However, the first story is acted out again and again when women become involved with a certain type of man. After the relationship ends, many women don't know what hit them—they simply can't make sense out of the experience. Other women may have a hint that the person they were dating was a self-centered jerk or a "player." The truth is that the first story describes the standard romantic relationship with a narcissistic man. The focus of this book is on relationships with these men. My hope is that by reading this book you will:

- Gain insight into narcissistic men and their approach to relationships
- Learn why you fall for narcissistic men
- Discover techniques for analyzing your current and past relationships
- Learn how to get over a past relationship with a narcissistic man
- Learn how to avoid narcissistic men in the future

Who are narcissists and why do psychologists use the term "narcissist" to describe arrogant and self-absorbed individuals? The term is derived from the ancient Greek myth of Narcissus. Narcissus was a terribly attractive young man who was seeking an equally attractive romantic partner. He wandered the earth looking for this partner, but no one was good enough for him. One of his potential loves was the beautiful and devoted nymph Echo. Echo adored Narcissus so much that she repeated ("echoed") every word that he said. Narcissus feigned attraction to Echo briefly, but then quickly lost interest in her. Echo, as her name implies, faded away. Eventually, Narcissus entered a dark forest where he found a pool of water. He looked into the pool and saw his own image staring back at him. Narcissus was in love! He was so captivated by his own beauty that he froze and died. At that spot by the water, a flower (the narcissus) grew.

The Greeks were amazingly accurate in their myth of Narcissus. This story captures the essence of the narcissistic men of today. Narcissists use people, but ultimately are interested only in themselves. The long-term outcome for the narcissist may be emotional emptiness, but in the short run they manage to hurt a great number of people.

The image of Narcissus appears in modern life as well. Many TV characters are narcissists. Television writers love a narcissist because he is colorful, makes a good "bad guy," and, for the sake of drama, can occasionally be transformed through the magic of TV into a nice and caring person. In fact, many of the things that make narcissists such great characters are also what make them such lousy relationship partners. Narcissists are outgoing, extroverted, confident, charming, ambitious, and often attractive. They are also self-centered, dishonest, uncaring, unfaithful, and deceptive. If narcissists were just plain bad, they would be much easier to hate. Instead, they have enough good traits to draw you in, and enough bad ones to make you miserable. Examples of narcissistic TV characters include several of the lead doctors in the TV series *Scrubs*, as well as, of course, Mr. Big from *Sex and the City*.

Narcissistic characters are even evident in many children's cartoons because they make such wonderful villains. My personal favorite is Gaston from Disney's *Beauty and the Beast*, who may be the most vain and self-absorbed character ever drawn. There is also, of course, the great Pepe le Pew who takes vanity to a whole other level.

The character of Mr. Big, played by Chris Noth in the TV series *Sex and the City*, possesses all the characteristics that can make relationships with narcissists so frustrating. On the one hand, he is handsome, charming, powerful, and wealthy. He even appears to have a caring relationship with Carrie (played by Sarah Jessica Parker). On the other hand, he really makes a mess of Carrie's life. He refuses to commit to her (although he has promised to on occasion), yet he takes up a relationship with her as soon as she enters a healthy relationship with another man. He marries a young, attractive "trophy wife" rather than Carrie, but then is unfaithful in his marriage. Through this combination of charm and dishonesty, he manages to keep emotional control of Carrie without ever committing. Even when he moves away from New York City, he leaves airline tickets for Carrie. Basically, Mr. Big manages to get everything he wants by manipulating Carrie, but he does it in such a charming and colorful way that Carrie (and the viewers) keeps wanting more of him. This being television, of course, at the end of the show Mr. Big finally turns into a good guy and Carrie is happy that she waited for him. Unfortunately, this is not what happens in typical relationships with narcissistic men.

There are many other figures in public life that match this portrait. Typical narcissists who come to mind may be cocky athletes, wealthy playboys, or sleazy politicians. We read about celebrity actors or CEOs (think Donald Trump) who marry strings of young "trophy" wives. We hear about politicians from both parties who spend as much time as possible pretending to be caring and sincere in front of the camera while at the same time cheating on their spouses with a variety of women. We see athletes and attorneys dressed up in five-thousand-dollar suits strutting around in front of the cameras like peacocks.

These examples of narcissistic men are easy to spot and usually easy to avoid. (Of course, plenty of women do not avoid them—a topic that will be covered later.) Unfortunately, the truth is that narcissistic men appear in all shapes and sizes. The key similarity is that he believes that he is (and wants to appear) special, intelligent, powerful, or successful and does not care about too much beyond that. You meet these men at work or out in the evening and may not recognize their narcissistic traits at first. Instead, he might seem charming, confident, attractive, and exciting. Unfortunately, the narcissistic side will usually emerge.

These are examples of the types of statements that I hear again and again from women in my research on narcissism:

- "He is arrogant, self-centered, and spoiled."
- "Every time we talk about something, the conversation turns back to him."
- "He thinks he is so smart, but now I know that he really isn't."

- "We have a lot of fun when we are out at parties, but we never spend too much time just talking."
- "He is always looking at other women, even when we are together."
- "Everything is about *him*."
- "He seemed great at first, but now I realize that he is just an arrogant jerk."

So, what exactly is it that makes someone a narcissist? In the simplest terms, narcissists have three key characteristics:

1. Narcissists have unrealistically high opinions of themselves.
2. Narcissists do not truly care about other people.
3. Narcissists use other people to maintain these high opinions of themselves.

Narcissists are said to love themselves. What does this mean? A narcissist thinks that he is special and unique. He feels entitled to all sorts of great things in life. He talks about himself. He thinks that he is smarter than other people. He assumes that other people will respect him and find him attractive. He constantly fantasizes about success and fame. He likes looking in the mirror.

At the same time, narcissists don't care so much about other people. He might seem charming, exciting, or dashing at first, but this behavior is usually temporary and only seen as long as it is effective in getting the narcissist what he wants. In reality, a narcissist cares primarily about himself and his success.

Finally, narcissists' actions are designed to maintain their positive self-image. Narcissists show off, thrive on being the center of attention, and seek to out-do others. He is competitive rather than cooperative and when he does not win, can get angry or violent. In short, a narcissistic man may seem charming or caring, but he will walk all over you to get what he wants.

I have heard people use many colorful metaphors to describe narcissists in action. One friend called these men "tornadoes" because they move through life sucking people in and leaving a path of destruction behind. The hurt that he inflicts on others is not important to the narcissist. One student used the expression "bubble people" because a narcissist seems to make everything that he gets close to (that gets "inside his bubble") about him. For example, a friend will discuss a problem and soon it will become a discussion of the narcissist's problem. Often the metaphor of a predatory animal is used to describe narcissists. Jimmy Buffett has a song called "Fins" that describes men at a bar circling a woman like sharks. I think that equating narcissists to the "sharks that can swim on land" may be unfair to sharks, but it does fit the description of narcissists as predators "on the prowl."

Finally, a fellow psychology professor was looking at some experimental results with me. In this study, we had narcissists work together on a project with a friend. At the end of the task, we told the pair that they had done well. We then asked each person who was responsible for the success of the pair. Most people in this situation will say something like, "Both my friend and I should share the credit for this success." Narcissists, of course, did not do this. Instead, the narcissist says something like, "I am responsible for the success; my friend did not have much to do with it at all." When I showed a graph of these results to my colleague, he thought for a half-second and then said, "These guys are just dicks!" This is a bit crass, but does get to the point.[1]

In psychological research, narcissism is measured with personality questionnaires. The most popular measure is the Narcissistic Personality Inventory, developed by Dr. Robert Raskin and colleagues. This is not a measure for diagnosing people as clinically disturbed. Rather, it for measuring narcissism in normal people—I use it all the time when doing research on college students. The following are some of the narcissistic items on the scale:[2]

- I know that I am a good person because everybody keeps telling me so.
- If I ruled the world, it would be a better place.
- I like to be the center of attention.
- I think I am a special person.
- I find it easy to manipulate people.
- I like to look at myself in the mirror.

What is interesting about these items is that they are not all terrible. There is nothing necessarily wrong, for example, with wanting to be the center of attention. One of the big problems with narcissism is what is missing— beliefs about close relationships. There is no mention of caring, intimacy, or closeness. Narcissists just don't take others' concerns into consideration.

At this point, I would like to pause briefly to describe the outline of this book. Chapter one will give you a "behind the scenes" look into narcissists' personalities. If you want to understand how narcissists operate in dating relationships, it is important to first understand how they see the world in general. (To the narcissist, romance is no different from business or sports.) Chapter two will describe narcissists' romantic relationships in detail: who they are attracted to, what they are looking for, and how they act. This chapter will provide you with a "narcissist's eye view" of relationships. The third chapter will answer a question that many women have wrestled with: If narcissists are such jerks, why do people such as myself ever date them? Chapter three also will explain why relationships with narcissists are so difficult to get over after they have ended. The fourth chapter will provide you with specific instructions for avoiding narcissists. It also will provide tools for analyzing your current relationship to see if you are dating a narcissist. Finally, chapter four will address the question: Can narcissists change? Chapter five will focus on the situation of women who repeatedly date narcissists. The majority of women I have talked to have had one or more bad experience dating narcissists, but other women keep doing it time and time again. In this chapter I provide concrete steps for avoiding narcissistic men.

Damn, I'm Good (but I'm no Mother Teresa)— Understanding the Difference Between Narcissism and High Self-Esteem

When speaking to people about narcissism, one of the biggest misconceptions that I run across is the belief that narcissism is simply very high self-esteem. In other words, if you took a person with high self-esteem and gave him even higher self-esteem, he would turn into a narcissist. This view is certainly understandable, but, fortunately, it is incorrect. Narcissism and high self-esteem are related but, as I will explain, they are two different creatures.

The truth is that everyone likes to feel good about himself or herself. In our society we call this having "high self-esteem." Self-esteem is something that we want and that we want our friends and romantic partners to have. We like people who are happy and feel relatively positively about themselves. Nobody likes to spend time with someone who is always self-critical or constantly needs emotional support.

Narcissists also report having high self-esteem. In fact, they do have high self-esteem. They really think that they are special and terrific individuals. Most people feel uncomfortable being filmed or even staring at themselves in a mirror. Not narcissists—they love it.[3] So why do we dislike narcissistic individuals but like people with high self-esteem? Let's begin by looking at self-esteem (often called "true," "healthy," "authentic," or "optimal" self-esteem).[1]

The good kind of self-esteem includes seeing yourself as "a person of worth" and "at least on an equal basis with others." This is a fundamental belief in one's value as a person. At the core, a person with high self-esteem feels that he is able to be loved, love others, and adapt to life's challenges. Below is a list of some items from the Rosenberg Self-Esteem Inventory.[5] This is the most popular self-esteem measure used by social scientists today. Note the differences in the measure of narcissism in the last section and the self-esteem scale.

- I feel that I'm a person of worth, at least on an equal basis with others.
- I feel that I have a number of good qualities.
- I am able to do things as well as most other people.
- I take a positive attitude toward myself.
- On the whole, I am satisfied with myself.

There are a couple of other things to keep in mind regarding self-esteem as opposed to narcissism. Genuine (or optimal) self-esteem has two important attributes. First, it is "non-contingent." A person with optimal self-esteem doesn't depend completely on factors in the environment to feel good about himself. Sure, he might feel bad when he botches an assignment at work or is disliked by someone he just met, but these feelings are temporary and do not damage his core positive belief in himself. At the same time, he does not need success at work or praise for his appearance in order to feel good about himself. He is not always looking for ways to "pump himself up." He already likes himself—this is the default setting. Second, optimal self-esteem is prosocial. In other words, a man with healthy high self-esteem does not set out to hurt others or need to constantly outperform others in order to feel good about himself. A man with high self-esteem does see himself as smart and successful, but he also sees himself as nice, easy to get along with, and moral. He likes and respects others (of course, optimal self-esteem is a goal; nobody is perfect in this regard).

Popular leading men in the movies are often portrayed as attractive and having high self-esteem without being narcissistic. Cary Grant, for example, often played characters who were high in self-esteem, attractive, but not narcissistic. The key is that these characters care about other people. These characters go out of their way to help—not hurt—others. Their main goal is not to forward their own image.

Now that we have a better idea of what true high self-esteem is, we can begin to understand what makes narcissists different. Narcissists and people with high self-esteem both have high opinions of themselves, but there are three important differences between these two groups.

First, narcissists' positive beliefs about themselves depend upon the social environment. What does this mean? Narcissists go through life looking for opportunities to shine. They want to win and look good doing it. Narcissists *need* to win or be admired in order to feel good about themselves. They *need* to be the best athlete, make the most money, or have the best car. More importantly, success is not enough. Narcissists *need* others around them to praise their victories and give them respect. Without others around to admire them, the success is meaningless.

Narcissists need to "toot their own horn." They do not have a deep and abiding sense of self-worth.

Women often tell me that their narcissistic partners are different in public than in private. In public they are often charming and confident; in private they may be nasty and dismissive. Narcissists show this difference in public and private in all sorts of ways. Two psychologists did a wonderful study on this. They had people who were and were not narcissistic come into the lab and play a game of darts in private. What the psychologists found was that the narcissists did a terrible job; narcissists weren't willing to put in the effort if there was no chance to be noticed for it. The psychologists then changed the study by leading the narcissists to believe that their performance on the dart game was part of a competition that would be known publicly. When the narcissists thought that they could achieve glory by winning, they tried much harder, and actually did better at the game. Narcissists love to look good.[6]

Second, narcissists' positive beliefs about themselves exist only in a handful of areas. This is because there are only a limited number of things that narcissists care about (hint: they don't care too much about *being* caring).[7] One of these things is their physical appearance. A narcissist is vain. A narcissist thinks he is good looking and wants everyone to notice him. At the extreme you get those guys who are human peacocks wearing expensive suits and far too many hair products.

What is really interesting about this is that narcissists are, in truth, no more physically attractive than other people—they just think and act as if they are. This is one reason why it is difficult to spot people who are vain. You can have one great-looking person who really does not care too much about his appearance and another really average-looking guy who thinks that he is God's gift to women. For this reason, I always warn women to be wary of men who spend more time in front of the mirror than they do.[8]

Narcissists also think that they are highly intelligent. They see themselves as smarter and more clever than others. This is very important to narcissists. As with looks, however, there is no actual difference in intelligence between narcissists and everyone else. Of course, there are narcissists who are highly intelligent. They will probably let you know this pretty quickly and may appear quite impressive. I have seen a narcissistic academic speak from time to time. He struts his stuff and appears quite knowledgeable, but his goal seems to be selling me on how smart he is and how important his ideas are. I have also seen lots of academics speak who are not narcissistic. These academics take a different approach. He or she seems genuinely focused on how interesting *the* (not *his or her*) ideas are. Non-narcissistic academics always want to get feedback and even criticism from the audience about the work.

Sometimes, of course, a narcissist's efforts to show how smart he is can be pretty funny. There was a character on a recent reality show, for example, who would constantly misuse large words. He apparently wanted desperately to appear sophisticated, but the truth was that he did not come across as very bright. (As an aside, narcissists can be found on many reality TV shows. The narcissist is drawn to the attention that being on TV will get him. On the shows, he or she tends to be vain, dramatic, and manipulative. Sometimes the narcissist will win, but usually the other contestants end up hating him or her. Of course, the drama that surrounds narcissists makes for great TV and because of this, the narcissist get lots of airtime and attention. Puck from the *Real World* was a character that seemed to have a lot of narcissistic traits, but was very entertaining to watch.)

Narcissists also see themselves as "special." They think that they are gifted, unique, or different from other people. They view themselves as special, their work as special, their needs as special, and their abilities as special. I spoke to a physician once who told me that he was like God because he saved lives. He never mentioned the role of the other physicians, the nurses, his teachers in medical school, his parents who paid for medical school, or even good luck. He thought that he was somehow given this gift of healing and that the world should acknowledge him for it. A physician with optimal high self-esteem would certainly feel good about saving a life, but would not forget the role that the rest of the world had in his success. In fact, his first thought would be for the well-being of his patient. Furthermore, he would be grateful for the opportunity to excel at his work and to help others.

Third, and I think this is crucial, narcissists generally do not see themselves as being caring, nice, or moral people. That is, narcissists think that they are better looking and smarter than others, but not more caring. There may be some exceptions to this rule where, for example, certain professional "crusaders" protest for the rights or salvation of others but in truth only care about their own egos. The rule, however, generally holds. If you think about this, there are some scary implications. People who believe that they are caring and moral usually try to do good things for others. We may want to steal the limelight (or a boyfriend) from our friends, but we know that it isn't moral and we don't want to hurt our friends. Therefore, we don't do it. Narcissists are not burdened by this baggage. You can tell them that they are mean, nasty, or unfair and it will not really bother them. Narcissists do not care that much about being nice people.

To summarize, narcissism simply is not very high self-esteem. It is a combination of excessive positive views of one's looks, intelligence, and dominance, with a general lack of caring for others. There is also another element of narcissism that is worth discussing. This is a sense of entitlement.

Entitlement: Narcissists' Secret Ingredient

The movie *Two Weeks Notice* was a story about a very wealthy, very self-involved, womanizing New York real estate mogul, George Wade (played by Hugh Grant) and his personal attorney, Lucy Kelson (played by Sandra Bullock). In the movie, Lucy agrees to work with George in order to stop a community center from being torn down and replaced by an enormous development. Although Lucy is a brilliant, Harvard-educated attorney, George treats her like a personal assistant, asking her to do a multitude of trivial personal tasks, often in the middle of the night. The low point comes when George sends Lucy an emergency page in the middle of a wedding where Lucy is the maid of honor. Lucy bolts from the ceremony to help with the emergency. It turns out, however, that all George wants is help picking out a suit. This is the last straw, and Lucy vows to quit her job. (Of course, this being Hollywood, Lucy falls in love with George's boyish charm and George has a great awakening and pledges his love to Lucy at the end of the film.)

Although the happy ending of this movie is not a great example of how narcissists behave, the scene at the wedding perfectly captures narcissists' least likeable trait: entitlement. Entitlement is more than just thinking you are great; entitlement has to do with thinking that you deserve more than other people—other people's needs don't even enter the equation. In the movie, when George needed someone to pick out his coat, he had no problem paging his attorney. The fact that she was in a wedding didn't even cross his mind. He needed a suit picked out and that was that. When Lucy was upset, George even seemed a bit confused—what was the problem? He simply needed a suit picked out. It was as if Lucy had no life outside George's. In a sense, it is as if other people existed simply for George.

Entitlement is a lot like selfishness and self-centeredness. It might be good to think about it as selfishness with an added kick. Selfishness simply involves taking more than your share of something, whether it is money, food, praise, whatever. People can be selfish and greedy for the simple reason that they want more. I may want a big piece of dessert, so I will cut myself the largest piece. You might call me a hog, but that is about it. What makes entitlement so infuriating is that people who feel entitled will take the bigger piece of cake and think that they *deserve* it. Somehow, because of their wealth, status, uniqueness, or God-given special place in the universe, they are entitled to the bigger piece. If you are in the way, that sucks for you.

To get a handle on the concept of entitlement, it may be worth looking at a psychological measure. This scale is known as the Psychological Entitlement Scale, and has done a great job at identifying highly entitled individuals.[9]

Please respond to the following items by writing the number that best reflects your own beliefs. Please respond using the following 7-point scale:

1 = strong disagreement

2 = moderate disagreement

3 = slight disagreement

4 = neither agreement nor disagreement

5 = slight agreement

6 = moderate agreement

7 = strong agreement

___ I honestly feel I'm just more deserving than others.

___ Great things should come to me.

___ If I were on the *Titanic*, I would deserve to be on the first lifeboat!

___ I demand the best because I'm worth it.

___ I do not necessarily deserve special treatment. (*reversed*)

___ I deserve more things in my life.

___ People like me deserve an extra break now and then.

___ Things should go my way.

___ I feel entitled to more of everything.

The average score on this scale is around twenty-nine for men and a couple of points lower for women. That means most people are slightly disagreeing with each of these statements. That is a good thing. Imagine a world in which everyone thought he or she was honestly more deserving than others. It would be a nightmare. There would be a lot of conflict at work and in relationships, and this conflict would be especially bad because everyone would think that he or she was on the side of the angels.

Fortunately, there are only a minority of people who go through life thinking that they are entitled to the success, status, and stuff. Unfortunately, however, it is these people who cause the problems. In one research study, for example, we wanted to see if highly entitled people would actually take candy from children. After measuring the entitlement scores of a group of people, the experimenter gave them a rather elaborate story. He held up a bucket of Halloween candy that he said was supposed to go to the children in the developmental lab. This was a plastic bucket with a black cat and witch on it. It had a large hand drawn sign, clearly done by a child, that said "Developmental Lab." Also, there was a sticky note on it that said "For Developmental Lab—Dr. C." Clearly, this was candy meant for children.

The question was, would the entitled people take the candy? The experimenter passed it around the room and secretly counted the amount of candy that people took. As we expected, the entitled people took the most candy. They felt that they deserved it and didn't seem to care that it was meant for the children.

In society, we see entitlement most clearly in the antics of certain celebrities, sports stars, and CEOs. Occasional cases in the media show somewhat stunning examples of this. My personal favorite is the former CEO of Tyco, Dennis Kozlowski, who was on trial for allegedly taking money from the company. During the trial, they released a video of the birthday party that he threw for his wife (using Tyco money, of course). The party was in Sardinia, and it was complete with scantily dressed actors running around in Ancient Greek costumes, a huge fireworks display, an ice sculpture of Michelangelo's *David* urinating vodka (truly a tasteful touch!), and Jimmy Buffett playing music. (C'mon, who doesn't deserve Jimmy Buffett to be flown halfway around the world for his party?)

What I liked about this party, beyond its utter cheesiness, was the fact that (a) the CEO used shareholder money to pay for it, and (b) he had the chutzpah or total lack of awareness to defend that decision. I don't care how some rich guy wants his vodka served. It is his money, and it keeps the ice sculptors working. Remember, however, that CEOs of public companies are not the owners, the public is. Those who are highly narcissistic often miss that distinction.

A second case is Michael Jackson, who just doesn't seem to get it. He invites boys over for slumber parties. Lo and behold, he gets accused of child molesting (this is years ago), someone gets paid off, and the case goes away. Apparently, Michael (who has his own kids, and a wife or two along the way) figures he would like to continue spending the night with boys. Surprise, surprise, he gets accused again of child molesting, and this time the case won't go away.

Now, if this isn't enough, here is where the real narcissism comes in. Michael jets into Santa Barbara to turn himself in and is handcuffed by the investigators. Most people who are handcuffed and made to do the "perp walk" try to hide the handcuffs because they are embarrassed or ashamed. Michael, in contrast, sticks his handcuffs out to show the world that he is being treated unfairly, like a common criminal. I am thinking, *You are spending the night with little boys. You are doing this even though you know that you have been accused of molestation before. What did you think was going to happen?* Michael, however, seems to see things differently. He is a big celebrity (the self-proclaimed "King of Pop") and he is entitled to spend the night with little boys if that is what he wants to do. People are simply envious of him and out to get him.

Now, to be fair to these and other entitled CEOs, star athletes, and music stars, it is understandable to some extent that they begin to feel entitled. Think about it, if you had 50 million dollars, thousands of adoring fans, and were surrounded by people who said, "How would you like your vodka served, Dr. Campbell?" you might start to take other people for granted. Not that this makes it right, but I can see it.

Unfortunately, entitled narcissists do not only exist in the upper classes. You probably work with two or three of these people. They don't have their own personal film crew, but think that they should have one. These entitled narcissists think they deserve things in the world to go their way. And you? You aren't even in the picture.

Mr. Fun

Imagine that you are at a big party. There is loud music, booze, and hundreds of important people from your community. You know several of the people in passing, but don't have any close friends there. How would you feel? Personally, I would be a bit uncomfortable and probably wishing I were out for a quiet meal with only a few friends. Most narcissists, however, wouldn't really mind this situation. He would look at this as a great opportunity to rub shoulders with the elite, drink a little too much, chat up a few women, and have a great time. In these settings, the narcissist's "Mr. Fun" personality can really be let out.

Narcissists, as I have described them in the previous sections, may sound like somewhat nasty people—and certainly can be. Fortunately (or unfortunately) there is another side to narcissists. If there wasn't this other side, they wouldn't be nearly as attractive as they are—you could simply avoid them. Those individuals with narcissistic qualities who live alone in cabins in Montana, write manifestos, and send out mail bombs, generally aren't attractive or on the dating scene. Sure, they think that they are smarter than everyone else and want to rule the world—like Dr. Evil from *Austin Powers*—but you are not likely to meet them at a party.

The narcissist that you are likely to meet can be fun and exciting to be around. You may feel special to be in his presence. He may be colorful and tell great stories. He can even make you feel good about yourself by acting in a charming and flattering way. Personally, I often enjoy hanging out with narcissists in social settings. They are confident, know lots of people, and seem to be where the action is.

This does not make sense on the surface. If narcissists only care about themselves and do not care about other people, why are they sometimes so much fun to be around? The answer has to do with narcissists' self-worth. Narcissists like to be surrounded by others because this helps narcissists to feel special and important. You see these guys at parties where they are surrounded by beautiful people. Narcissists love this. It's as though high school has never ended. I heard a great story from a woman recently. She dated a narcissistic guy in college, but hadn't seen him in over a year. When she ran into him at a bar, he put on a big show. He bought a round of drinks for all her friends and handed out business cards from his new company that listed him as CEO. (It turns out that there were only two people in the company!) All her friends were really impressed at his generosity; they thought he was a pretty terrific guy. This, of course, is exactly what the narcissist was looking for. In short, narcissists are often more social than others. It's even possible that the social scene can be like a drug to them. They get so excited by the social scene that they feel a "rush." This rush makes them even more cocky. They feel popular, important, powerful, and desirable.[10]

The basic recipe for narcissists' "Mr. Fun" personality has four ingredients: extroversion, confidence, charm, and, commonly, color.

Narcissists generally are extroverted and outgoing. They prefer social interactions with lots of people rather than intimate conversations with a few friends. They are energetic and seem to be further energized by social contact. They look outward rather than inward. The classic example of extroversion can be been seen in certain politicians. Some politicians can meet hundreds of people in a day, and rather than get exhausted, they get more and more energized. The politician smiles and makes each person feel like he or she is important. Politicians love making the rounds at cocktail parties filled with strangers. They appear on talk shows week after week. Most people are exhausted just thinking about this lifestyle. Extroverts love it. Why are narcissists extroverted? I think that in part they are just born that way, but it may be that they learn to be extroverted in order to get the attention that they want.

Narcissists also are very confident. Many people feel anxious speaking in public or meeting strangers. They worry that they might make a bad impression or that their speech will be not be liked. This is so difficult for some people that they actually develop phobias about being in public or speaking in public. In fact, public speaking is right up there with heights and spiders (and even death!) in the list of people's biggest fears. You even now see TV ads for pills that claim to cure social anxiety.

Narcissists are not at all like this. Instead of being afraid of being negatively evaluated (who would not love them?), narcissists see social situations as a place where they can excel or be admired. Narcissists love the limelight.

The next ingredient in narcissists' "Mr. Fun" personality is their occasional charm. (I say *occasional* because sometimes they are arrogant jerks—whatever works for them at the time.) Narcissists have several attributes that lead to this charming behavior. First, narcissists are good talkers. They are practiced at social interactions and know how to appear impressive. They may take on a "smooth-talking" style, which is possible because of their lack of social anxiety. They are actors who are good at putting on a show. Narcissists will order the correct drink at the correct bar wearing the correct clothes at the correct time using the correct popular terminology.

Narcissists also are very accomplished at flattery. Narcissists live in a world where flattery is important and they know how to apply this flattery to other people. In other words, narcissists know how to stroke people's egos. Of course, narcissists are likely to compliment you on the things that are important to them: looks, intelligence, specialness, and social skills. If narcissists want to, they can make you feel special, attractive, and talented.

Finally, narcissists can make you feel important by sharing the limelight a little bit. Narcissists will let you briefly step into their world and get the sense of importance that the narcissist feels. You can drive in the narcissist's car, hang out with his important friends, and feel part of his important world. The movie *The Talented Mr. Ripley* is a great example of this. Matt Damon's character got to live in the narcissists' world for a brief time, and he loved it.

Basically, narcissists' charm works by tapping into the narcissistic needs of others. Almost everyone has a hint of egotism in her character. We like to feel special and important; we may even get hooked on it. Narcissists can see that element and make it work. It can be intoxicating to be with a narcissist when the act is working. Of course, there are other times when a narcissist's charm does not work—for example, when your needs are the opposite of his needs, a different person will emerge. When you see the narcissist's act in the harsh light of truth, he may take on a very different character. All sorts of words starting with "S" come to mind: slick, slimy, slippery, snake-like, and scum. I talk about some of these traits in the next sections.

The final ingredient in narcissists "Mr. Fun" personality is color. Narcissists can be very colorful individuals at times. Sometimes they are described as "personalities." By this I mean that the things they do often appear larger than life. They sometimes seem more interesting and engaging than the things that mere mortals do. Douglas MacArthur, one of America's greatest generals, had this colorful quality. He wore aviator sunglasses, smoked a large corn-cob pipe, and made bold statements such as the famous, "I shall return!" These colorful qualities resulted in large amounts of attention and admiration from the public, as well as from his troops. His arrogance (which was largely deserved—he was a heck of a leader), however, cost him his job when he publicly disagreed with President Truman over war policy.[11]

Today, it is often CEOs and other corporate leaders who have these colorful qualities. Larry Ellison, currently CEO of Oracle computer, is known as having a large ego. His biography is titled, *The Difference Between God and Larry Ellison*—the punch line being, "God doesn't think he's Larry Ellison." Ellison is known not just for being a highly competitive and successful businessman, but also sailing in the Americas Cup, building an enormous Japanese garden, wearing a trademark double-breasted suit and black

T-shirt, and being a notorious womanizer. Compare that to more successful but less colorful Bill Gates, who is known for playing bridge, being nerdy, and having more money than anyone on the planet. Not too colorful. Who would you want to party with?

Do Not Look at the Man Behind the Curtain (or, Maintaining the Narcissist's Illusion)

There is the old tale of the emperor who had no clothes, but walked around as if he were wearing a beautiful garment. All his subjects confirmed that he in fact did have on a lovely robe. One day, however, a small child blurted out that the emperor was naked. Suddenly the spell was broken and everyone saw the emperor for what he was: buck naked.

Narcissists are a lot like the fabled emperor. A narcissist sees himself as wearing a beautiful garment containing his physical appearance, talents, and specialness. This situation is an inherently tricky one. There are people in the world who might not see the narcissist's unique and special talents. The primary goal of the narcissist is to prevent this from happening. To do this, he must either spend time with people who see his clothes, or punish those who do not.

Another character who comes to mind is the wizard in *The Wizard of Oz*. He portrayed himself as an imposing power and scared the population into obedience. The truth eventually came out when Dorothy went to find the real wizard. His great line was, "Pay no attention to that man behind the curtain!" Dorothy did. What she saw was a little man holding a series of levers that controlled his powerful public image. Like the wizard, narcissists create the illusion of specialness. They do not want anyone to look too deeply behind the curtain. Unlike the wizard, it is not that narcissists are weak or little deep down inside. Instead, they are just like everyone else. Most of us are content being like other people—for a narcissist, this is a terrible state of affairs.

Narcissists have some advantages over the emperor or the wizard. Narcissists have a bag of psychological tricks and tactics at their disposal. Psychologists have identified two groups of these tactics. These may be thought of as creating an inflated and positive *inner world* and developing an inflated and positive *outer world*.

Narcissists have an active inner life. They like to fantasize and in their fantasies they act out a highly positive self-image.[12] They dream of fame, power, intelligence, and success. I remember a guy I met once who fit many of the characteristics of a narcissist. He was not particularly successful, nor was he very attractive. The latter was due to his penchant for sitting on the couch and eating bacon double-cheese burgers from In and Out. Despite his obvious failings, he thought that he was smarter than the masses. Each day he would watch *Jeopardy* on TV. He would call the contestants idiots and at the end of the game say that he won and that the money "should have been mine." He was clearly meeting his narcissistic needs in his fantasy life. To the best of my knowledge, he never actually tried out for *Jeopardy*— or got off the couch! The Internet has made it much easier for people to have narcissistic fantasy lives. All you need to do is read bulletin boards to see the egotistical and angry posts left by many anonymous individuals.

Narcissists also use their social world to keep feeling great. We all get feedback from the world about our abilities—sometimes we win, sometimes we lose. Narcissists distort feedback from the world to fit their positive self-images more than do others. One of their favorite tricks is what psychologists call the *self-serving bias*. This means taking credit for successful outcomes and blaming the environment for failing outcomes. If a narcissist does well on a project, he will think, "I am a genius." If he fails, however, he will blame his boss, the co-workers, the alignment of the planets—anything but his own inadequacies.

We might not be aware of it, but we all play a role in creating our social world. We can go to church or go out drinking; we can spend time with people who genuinely care about us, or people who are popular but who put us down; we can dress in strange clothes and get tattoos on our arms or we can dress like everyone else. All our choices affect the world that we experience.

Narcissists attempt to use and create a social world that will keep them looking and feeling good about themselves. Narcissists select people to socialize with who will make them feel popular and special. In high school, when adolescents are trying to form their identities, it is important to hang out with the "cool kids." By doing so, the adolescents themselves feel cool. Narcissists as adults still act like high school kids. They want to be seen with other special and popular people. They may even become "hangers-on," or groupies, to celebrities. They may dress in stylish clothes and put on a cool front. Anything to be special. I saw a movie, *Phone Booth*, which highlighted this narcissistic front. Colin Farrell plays a sleazy, manipulative, and dishonest celebrity publicist who acts as if he is connected to the celebrity scene in New York. He even had a kid that would follow him around holding his multiple cell phones. He would go to a certain phone booth every day to call a potential girlfriend and keep the records of the phone calls away from the eyes of his wife. The illusion finally breaks down when he is caught in the phone booth by a serial killer. (Of course, this being Hollywood, he ends up having a breakthrough and going back to his wife.)

Sometimes no "cool kids" can be found and narcissists are forced to socialize with people who are not up to their standards. When this happens, the narcissist may name-drop. He will talk about the time he spent with a famous or popular individual. "I remember that party that I was at last summer with Matt Damon." Of course, these stories may be gross exaggerations or outright lies, but they still have the effect of inflating the narcissist's self-image.

A friend of mine told me about a trip that he was on to Europe once with a group of other Americans. One of the men in the group was an obvious narcissist. At every stop, he felt that he needed to tell them about his own experiences. He apparently had studied art in Italy, attended the Sorbonne, and run with the bulls in Pamplona. He liked my friend as long as he acted interested in his stories, but everyone on the trip became increasingly annoyed with him. No one actually told him to shut up to his face, but it was a popular topic of conversation when he was not around!

Narcissists also like to be the center of attention when they are in social situations. To draw attention to himself, he may use exaggerated movements, flash money, or speak loudly. He also may try to dominate conversations so that others are forced to listen to them. Often narcissists are very good at this, and you might not see it happening.[13]

A narcissist's favorite topic is, of course, himself. Two psychologists did a clever study that really shows narcissists in action. Individuals took a narcissistic personality test (the one described previously) and then were led into a room with a tape recorder. They were asked to talk about any topic they wanted: movies, books, politics, sports, etc. There is a whole universe of interesting things to discuss. Out of the entire universe of topics, narcissists talked about themselves.[14]

Finally, narcissists love to show off. He likes to brag about or display his talents, skills, possessions, or good looks. He may perform, describe a great success, or parade around in an expensive outfit and pose in various places. Competition is a place where narcissists can really shine. Any competitive endeavor will give a narcissist the chance to both look good and gain power or status over others. He likes to win in intellectual games, athletics, and any other contest—especially when the victory is made public.

The bottom line is that the narcissist creates a world where he (not necessarily you or anyone else) can look good and feel good. He orchestrates his entire life in order to feel special and unique. He selects the people he wants to be with, talks about the subjects he wants to talk about, and tries to look good doing it. This takes a tremendous amount of effort, but it is the only way that the emperor can keep his beautiful clothes or the wizard can keep his powerful exterior. Of course, even the narcissist's perfect world sometimes crumbles.

When the Bubble Bursts (or, What Happens When the Truth Breaks Through)

Nobody likes to be criticized or rejected, but it happens. The key is how we respond to it. The most positive response, of course, is to stay calm and rational. If the criticism is useful and accurate, we may want to pay attention; if the criticism is hostile and misguided, we may want to ignore it. Rarely does it make sense to get upset or emotional. This mature and rational response to criticism is difficult. Another way to respond is to get depressed. Psychologists call this *internalizing*. Our first impulse is to blame ourselves for the situation and feel sad, anxious, or guilty. This is not such a good way of dealing with criticism, but at least nobody gets hurt. Finally, we can *externalize*. Basically, we can get angry and lash out at the criticizer. This is the choice that narcissists make.

I heard a story from a colleague once about a narcissistic artist. Like any good narcissist, Brad thought that he was extremely talented and that soon the entire world would recognize his true genius. Unfortunately for him, there are many great artists in the world and Brad was not one of them. He managed to keep his illusions alive for many years. He surrounded himself with a string of groupies whom he convinced that he was the next Picasso. He paraded around in a suave French beret and scarf, and he spoke at length about the meaning behind his work—cats symbolize man's quest for inner knowledge, shoes represent a mother image, blah, blah, blah....

Unfortunately, illusions can last only so long. Reality managed to creep into his perfect world in the form of bad reviews and financial failures. The press did not like his work and he could not sell enough art to make a living. At first he ignored these messages. Instead, he got by thanks to the adoration (and financial support) of a small number of admirers. When this did not work, he would burst into occasional fits of rage. He would yell at newspaper stories or scream about stupid art collectors. He managed to blame everyone and everything else for his problems. When the anger and blame did not work, he really began to break down. He drank too much and sank into long depressions. Finally, he went into therapy to deal with the depression (but not the narcissism, which he still had not recognized).

The trials and tribulations of the narcissistic artist are a good example of those times when narcissists' illusions break down. The response of narcissists to this information includes anger, blame, and, on rare and extreme occasions, depression. You generally don't want to be around when a narcissist crashes. This aggressive behavior on the part of narcissists is not difficult to find. In fact, it can be rather easily demonstrated in a laboratory setting. Two well-known academic psychologists, Brad Bushman from the University of Michigan and Roy Baumeister from Florida State University, conducted a study that very clearly reveals narcissistic aggression. These researchers had students write an essay on a creative topic. Next came the ego threat. The students were told that their essay was very poorly written. They told the students something like, "This is one of the worst essays that I have ever read!" (Every student got the same false feedback.) Finally, aggression was measured. You can't actually allow someone to hurt another person in a psychology study, but you can allow him to *think* that he is hurting another person. In this study, the narcissists and non-narcissists were given the chance to blast the person who criticized them with painfully loud white noise. [15]

Narcissists approached this part of the experiment with gusto! After receiving the bad review of their creative work, the narcissistic students were thrilled with the chance to get back at the person who criticized them. They blasted her with extremely loud noise in an effort to cause her pain. In contrast, the students who were not narcissists did not blast with very loud noise. They were not as threatened by the criticism.

This research teaches us a frightening lesson: If you criticize narcissists and threaten their inflated view of themselves, they are likely to attack. Sometimes this involves verbal assaults and sometimes it involves physical assaults. Narcissists will punish those who do not support their distorted vision of the world. A great movie scene about narcissistic aggression involved Joe Pesci playing a mobster in the movie *Goodfellas*. In the scene, a waiter said that Pesci was funny. Pesci became furious— "What do you mean, I'm funny? Am I a clown? Am I here to amuse you?" He then shot the waiter.

The other way to anger narcissists is to reject them. The spate of school shootings in this country at places like Columbine were often initiated by some experience of social rejection. The shooters usually felt that someone or some group in the school (jocks, preppies, etc.) didn't give them the attention and respect that they deserved. Of course, lots of kids get rejected at school, but arrogant, narcissistic kids are more likely to respond with violence. The perpetrators of Columbine, for example, were far from mild-mannered kids with low self-esteem. Instead, they spent their free time video-taping themselves shooting guns and pretending to kill people. They even had plans for the movie that would be made of the shootings, with the aspiration that Spielberg or Tarantino would film it.

This type of group violence can also be shown in a lab. In one study, groups of five people would show up to the lab. Each of them would be asked to pick two people who they liked and respected to be in the group. Some of the individuals would then be separated from the group and given some bad news—nobody had picked them for the group. These rejected people would then be given the task of setting the volume of the white noise blasts used in the study. They could have the four people in the group who rejected them experience loud and painful white noise blasts, or quiet and painless white noise blasts. Just like the kids at Columbine, the narcissists who were rejected would crank up the volume and blast away.[16]

Anger often works for narcissists. They manage to keep feeling good about themselves and at the same time keep others from criticizing them. People learn to "walk on eggshells" around narcissists. Narcissists also may combine anger with charm. They will be angry and aggressive enough to intimidate those around them into keeping quiet. They will then turn on the charm to keep people from leaving.

In the face of sustained criticism from a group of sources, however, the narcissistic aggression trick may stop working. Like Brad the artist, narcissists may not be able to ward off criticism from various people day after day. In these extreme cases, a narcissist can actually fall into depression. He may still blame others for his problems, but he feels depressed nonetheless.

Narcissists are generally pretty inadequate at dealing with these episodes of depression. The easy thing to do would be to realize, "Hey, I've been an arrogant jerk my whole life and I have treated other people poorly. I will change and try to be nice to others. I will work hard at my job rather than thinking that I am a legend." This doesn't happen very often. Narcissists are way too committed to their illusion of specialness. So instead of treating the real problem, narcissists treat the symptoms (i.e., the depression).

There are lots of positive long-term solutions to treating depression. The best seems to be a combination of cognitive-behavioral therapy and antidepressants. There are lots of short-term "solutions" for treating depression as well. Some popular ones are drugs, drinking, and binge eating. The reason that people prefer the short-term solutions is that they are easy to use and immediately effective. People will quickly feel better after three martinis. Short-term solutions also postpone the pain of dealing with the real problem. The downside of short-term solutions is that they make the problem worse in the long run. The next day, you've got a hangover and the actual problem still remains unresolved.

The narcissist is better at short-term solutions. He is too cocky to take advice from others. He is also far from willing to make changes that may threaten the illusions that have sustained him over the years. Instead, a narcissist may binge on alcohol or illicit drugs. He likes the sensations involved in drugs and drink—it is fun and exciting. He may binge on brief sexual encounters or one night stands that offer him fleeting ego boosts. He may go on a party binge combining both of these elements for days or weeks at a time. A narcissist will not deal with the real problem.

Women often walk away from their experiences with narcissists confused. She may say that the guy seemed to have "two sides to him" or "a dark side." At first she thought the narcissist was really outgoing and charming. When pressure was put on, however, an entirely different person emerged—someone who was self-destructive, violent, or scary. The charming, outgoing narcissist is the one who is getting everything that he wants. He is manipulating his social world to make himself feel special and important. The dark side of the narcissist emerges when things do not go his way and when he cannot charm, blame, or bluff his way out of it. Mr. Hyde emerges when the bubble bursts. We will return to this issue again, but first we will to address the most-commonly asked six questions about narcissism.

Six Other Questions about Narcissists

Whenever narcissism is discussed, several questions are repeated again and again.

Question 1: Where does narcissism come from?

Women often ask me: What made so-and-so a narcissist? Did he have a bad childhood? Was he born that way? My initial response has always been to think of an old parable the Buddha told. It goes something like this: There is a man wounded by an arrow. He is dying, but before he gets a doctor, he wants to know what kind of bow shot him, who made the arrow, and what type of wood the arrow was made from. The point is that the immediate concern should be the current situation; where the problems started originally have very little importance and they won't change anything.

However, I also understand the need to make sense out of things, so I will try to answer the question as best I can. It is tough to give a definitive answer, because there are several ideas about where narcissism comes from, but not many good studies have been done. Recently, however, a colleague of mine, Dr. Bobby Horton, completed a large study of high school kids and children that sheds some important light on the development of narcissism. What is interesting about this study is that he was able to distinguish the parenting that led to narcissism and to healthy self-esteem. The short version is that narcissists' parents did care about them; however, they did two things that were in direct contrast to the parents of those with healthy self-esteem. First, narcissists' parents were much more permissive. Parents of narcissists let their kids get away with things and didn't do a good job keeping tabs of them. A sad example of this is the kids involved in the Columbine shootings. They were able to run around their house, and town, shooting guns and making violent movies. In contrast, parent of kids with high self-esteem keep an eye on them—they know where they are and what they are doing.

Second, the parents of narcissists are interested in their children, but in a very "contingent" way. What I mean by this is that these parents will support and celebrate their children when they perform well, but may withdraw love when they do not. I always think of the parents you see at football games who are proud as can be of their sons when they win, but scream at them, the coach, and the other fans when they do poorly. In contrast, the parents of kids with high self-esteem love them unconditionally. They will, of course, punish them for bad behavior, but the love they have for their children does not depend on their success in sporting events.

If you put these two ideas together, you get some idea of what can set someone on the path to narcissism. As a child, you learn that you can do whatever you want. You also learn that people will pay attention to you when you succeed. There isn't a core basis of warmth or intimacy in your relationship with your parents. So, you continue this pattern when you are older—do what you want, and project the image of a winner.[17]

Of course, there is more to the development of narcissism (or any other trait for that matter) than parenting. Parents get more of their share of the blame for their kids. We all know cases where one kid is a disaster and the other turns out to be terrific. There is probably a big genetic component. Also, culture and the social situation play a big part as well. I will talk more about that later in the book.

Question 2: What is the difference between narcissism and narcissistic personality disorder?

The vast majority of what is written in the popular literature on narcissism is actually about narcissistic personality disorder (also called "NPD"). This is considered a disorder that shows up in less than one percent of the population. Basically, NPD is very rare. In this book, I am writing primarily about narcissism as a basic personality trait (although I will talk a little bit about NPD). There are a whole lot of narcissistic people out there, and you are a lot more likely to end up dating a narcissist than someone with full-blown NPD.

So, what is the difference between your everyday narcissist and someone with NPD? The simple answer would be that it is a question of extremity: NPD is just very extreme narcissism. There is certainly some truth to this, but I think there is another answer as well. I think people with NPD have some other problem. Maybe they are depressed; maybe they have failed too many times; maybe they are just bad at being narcissists. You can think about it this way: If you were a narcissist, why would you ever see a shrink? You're attractive, popular, and special. People love and admire you. You are smarter and more powerful than most of the losers in the world. You have high self-esteem and are happy. Basically, you are doing just fine in this life and, if other people don't see that, they can kiss your butt. Seriously, you have to be a really lame narcissist (or, in rare cases, very highly self-aware) to see a therapist. Consequently, the narcissists that therapists see are primarily the failed ones. They are narcissists who can't keep up with their own illusions. This is, in my opinion, why most of the popular books on narcissism (as well as much of the psychiatric literature) talk about narcissists being "fragile," depressed, or feeling empty. Unfortunately, this just isn't the case.[18]

Question 3: I have always heard that narcissists really hate themselves deep down inside. Is this true?

There is a very popular notion that narcissists, even though they may act like they are confident and have high self-esteem, actually hate themselves deep down inside. That is why they get so angry when people criticize them. I don't know where this idea came from originally, probably the psychoanalytic literature. What I do know is that it doesn't really make sense.

Let me give you a little thought experiment. Let's say you went back in time and met a great Egyptian Pharaoh. Instead of bowing like everyone else in the chamber, you instead walked up to the Pharaoh, spit at him, and called him a loser. What would happen? He would probably have his guards grab you and toss you in prison. Is this because he is insecure and depressed deep down inside? No, it is because he is the Pharaoh and you challenged him, so he had to respond.

Now you might argue that, well, maybe he is really insecure deep down, and that is why he makes everyone bow, or whatever. I say: When in doubt, think about the animal kingdom. Imagine you are sitting with a troop of gorillas in an African jungle. The dominant male in the group, a silverback called Gus, is sitting under a tree eating a banana. You, knowing that apes can't hate themselves deep down inside, run up to Gus and steal his banana. Would Gus not respond because he doesn't hate himself deep down inside? No, Gus would probably smack you upside the head and take the banana back.

The point is that narcissists are in their own minds like Pharaohs or Alpha Apes. They think they are the dominant ones. If this dominance is threatened, they will act to restore it. This is not because they secretly hate themselves deep down inside; it is because they are arrogant jerks.[19]

Question 4: Are men more narcissistic than women?

Men are definitely more narcissistic than women. The difference, however, is small. It is not that all men are narcissistic and no women are. Rather, on average, men are a little bit more narcissistic than women. This seems to be the case around the world—not just in the United States.

The follow-up question, of course, is why are men more narcissistic? The answer is that it seems to be part of a much bigger gender difference. Men have higher self-esteem than women; men are more self-serving; men are also more individualistic in their relationships. Men get angry more than women do and are more violent and drink more. Men commit more crimes and are far more likely to end up in prison. Women are more relationship-focused than men are. They tend to be more conscientious and do better academically. They are also more anxious and depressed. In short, men have a more narcissistic, individualistic, selfish, and sometimes angry approach to the world; women have a less narcissistic, more relationship-oriented, selfless, and anxious approach to the world. These differences are small, but pervasive.

Of course, the big question is where do these differences come from? Some people say culture and society, others say biology. I imagine that it is a little of both.

Question 5: Are there different types of narcissists?

When I talk to people about narcissism, I hear two basic questions about types of narcissists. First, some people will say, "I knew a guy who is a lot like what you describe, except that he was quiet and introverted." or "he didn't think he was smart, but he thought that he was a great athlete." Does a narcissist have to have all the qualities that you describe? Second, I have had several people ask me about specific types of narcissists. One woman, for example, emailed me and said that her husband was a "narcissist of the trickster type." I have seen this and other "types" all over the Internet.

My own feeling is that personality is largely a matter of degrees. Many narcissists don't have every feature described in this book—these are just the norms or averages. For example, I have had several women married to scientists tell me that their husbands were narcissists, but were introverted (quiet and withdrawn) instead of extroverted. This makes sense to me. Being a scientist can be a pretty introverted existence, but we sure have narcissists among us. If we were talking about salesmen, however, I would expect there to be a lot more extroversion.

So, I hesitate breaking down narcissists into types. It may be useful for some people to do this—and if it is useful, I say go for it. This is especially true when making diagnoses in clinical settings, where everything is defined by types.[20]

Question 6: Do people get less narcissistic as they get older?

Getting older has a lot of drawbacks, but it does have some benefits as well. One of those is that we all mellow out a bit. Narcissism, for example, appears to drop as people get older, perhaps as much as 25 percent.[21] A lot of related things drop as well. As people get older they are less likely to have all sorts of mental illness, and they are less likely to be criminals.

What this means for narcissism, of course, is that the most narcissistic people you find will be young males in high school and in college, followed by those in their late twenties and thirties. In fact, high school age males can be so narcissistic that the American Psychiatric Association warns against diagnosing them as having narcissistic personality disorder.

Why the high narcissism scores in adolescence? My guess is that it is a combination of several different things. Young males can be as cocky as they want because they really have nothing but potential. They can brag about what winners they will be when they get older and believe it. This is a lot harder when you are stuck in a middle management position at age fifty-five. Also, you are more attractive when you are young. At eighty years old, you can get eighteen face lifts and dress like Justin Timberlake, but it is tough to keep the appearance of youth. Also, there are some basic developmental changes that take place at different times. Young males are trying to establish an identity and career, which may fit with narcissism. When men reach middle age, they often reach a point where they want to give something back to the next generation. This is not very compatible with narcissism. Finally, there may be underlying hormonal shifts that account for some of the change. As men get older, their testosterone levels drop. Testosterone makes people energized, focused, confident, and also easy to anger. (This happens to women as well as to men—it is pretty cool. I talked to a researcher who wore a testosterone patch for a week. She described her entire mindset changing in a more individualistic and more focused direction.) It is not that testosterone is the "narcissism hormone," but it does lead to a lot of behaviors and experiences that would make narcissism more likely.[22]

Of course, there are definitely people who manage to stay narcissistic throughout their entire lives. I think (and most clinicians would agree) that it gets harder and harder to be narcissistic as you get older. At least, it becomes more and more pathetic. It is one thing to see a twenty-five-year-old with a leased Mercedes lying to a young woman; it is another thing to see a sixty-five-year-old doing the same thing.

We have spent this chapter describing narcissists. These descriptions and examples are by necessity extreme. Not all narcissists have all of these characteristics. Narcissists often are subtle and difficult to spot in their behaviors. Nevertheless, I hope that at least on occasion you recognized some of these narcissistic features in people who you have heard of or who you have known.

The following chapters of this book deal with the central issue of narcissists in romantic relationships. As you may have guessed, narcissists' self-centered approach to the world does tremendous damage to their romantic relationships. You will learn how narcissists approach their relationships, including specific steps for identifying narcissists before you date them and for determining whether you are currently dating (or have dated) a narcissist. You will also learn why narcissistic men can be so attractive—even though they make such lousy boyfriends. Finally, you will be given techniques for avoiding relationships with narcissistic men in the future.

Chapter Two

Narcissists in Relationships

To defeat the enemy you need to know how the enemy thinks. The goal of this chapter is to do just that—to help you understand how narcissists approach and experience romantic relationships. This is difficult because we often make the assumption that other people are like us, with the same thoughts, feelings, and motivations. This is not a good assumption to make when dealing with a narcissist.

The "narcissist's-eye-view" of romantic relationships in this chapter is the result of several large research studies conducted on hundreds of people. It also takes into account several clinical accounts of narcissists as well as anecdotal evidence.

There are several important "take home" messages in this chapter, but two that I find particularly important are the following:

1. From the narcissist's perspective it is all about *his* (not your) needs and goals, which are basically status, esteem, power, freedom, pleasure, and sex.

2. Narcissists are not that interested in intimate or caring relationships. It is just not that important to them to be emotionally close to someone else.

These two themes appear in all aspects of narcissists' relationships. We'll start with narcissists' use of romantic relationships in their quest for social status and esteem.

Being the Top Dog (or, It's All About Winning)

When most people think about dating, several images come to mind. These include closeness, intimacy, friendship, support, passion, and romance. Relationships are not like sporting events or business ventures. Ideally, they offer many positive things that are not available in other parts of your life. You generally don't go to work for social support or intimacy and you don't look to relationships for success, competition, or winning.

Narcissists, unfortunately, are not like other people. For narcissists, the goal of romantic relationships is the same as that of any other social relationship. *Narcissists want to win and look good doing it.* Narcissists see relationships as a place to be top dog, head honcho, conquering hero, and all-around legend.

This concept can be very difficult to understand for those who are not narcissists. For most people, relationships are great precisely because they are *not* about winning or competing. Relationships are a place where you can let your guard down and actually be yourself. Relationships should provide balance or sanctuary from a hectic and competitive public life. Narcissists, however, thrive in the competitive, dog-eat-dog world and see their relationships as just another extension of this. How do narcissists use relationships to maintain their private and public image as winners?

To start with, winners need trophies. A trophy shows you and others that you have won a competition. Narcissists are especially interested in obtaining and displaying their trophies. Relationships provide access to a special type of trophy: a popular and good-looking romantic partner.

Everyone knows the story. A successful executive or movie actor divorces his wife of twenty years and parades around town with a model who is twenty years younger. People look at this person and say something like, "There goes Charles and his new trophy wife."

Now, why did Charles marry this woman? It is certainly not about emotional intimacy. How much does this successful and accomplished man have in common with this woman at the start of her career? It is probably not even about passion—passion is sustained by increased intimacy.[1] Rather, the reason for Charles's new "trophy" marriage is that he thinks it makes him look like a winner. He can attract the affection of a young, pretty woman and that means that he must be pretty special. He will get admiring looks from his colleagues and people at parties, and this will further reaffirm his own self-image as a powerful, attractive, and successful man. The trophy spouse is no different in this regard from an expensive watch, expensive car, or oversized home. Last week I read a magazine article about Donald Trump that included pictures of his ex-wives and girlfriends. He has brought the trophy thing to a whole new level.

There is another type of trophy narcissists seek that is less apparent to observers—the "trophy family." These narcissists do not run off with women half their age; rather, they project their image as winners by having a "perfect" wife and family. They will go to great lengths to talk about how successful their children are and how perfect their summer vacation was.

I remember a man I met once at a party. He spent half an hour explaining to me that his son had chosen Harvard over Princeton because Princeton was "overrated." Now, there is nothing wrong with being proud of your children's accomplishments. Getting into a great university is a real accomplishment that takes a lot of hard work and persistence, and this work should be lauded by society. This man, however, was not proud of his son's hard work. He was not even proud of his son's success. Instead, he was proud of *himself* for his son's accomplishment. He was using the fruits of his child's labor as a way to feed his own ego. If he had been showing me his new car, he would have used the same tone of voice and expected the same admiration on my part. I agreed with him that Harvard was indeed a great university (and it is), but inside I felt sorry for his son.

I actually did my doctoral dissertation on the topic of narcissists' "trophy" relationships. I asked hundreds of people what they wanted from a romantic relationship. Over and over, it was clear that narcissists wanted someone who was attractive, popular, and important—even if that person was not at all interested in a caring or emotionally intimate relationship. The narcissists were drawn to these people because they gave the narcissists status and esteem, and also because the narcissists (who considered themselves to be very successful and attractive) felt similar to the trophies. In one simple study, I just asked people to list the most important trait in a romantic partner. My favorite answer from a narcissist was "pulchritude." For those of you who didn't just finish studying for the SATs, this is a rarely used term for beauty. The narcissist thus had a two-part message in his response: 1. I like beautiful women. 2. I am smarter than you, because I use words like pulchritude.[2]

In short, relationships for narcissists are just another avenue for gaining esteem and attention. In the extreme, I have even heard stories of narcissistic boyfriends picking out clothes for their girlfriends before going to parties. They hoped that their girlfriends would stand out—and draw attention to the narcissist! They may appear interested in their girlfriends or their kids, but narcissists' interest ends when they stop gaining esteem and attention.

It is not always easy to see narcissists' use of their partners as trophies. This is especially true for those who are dating the narcissists—the "trophies" themselves. Why? First, when you're being treated like a trophy, it can be exciting and superficially increase your self-esteem. Imagine walking into a party on Trump's arm and having everyone look at you. It would feel good. Second, it is easy to mistake your partner's efforts to display you publicly as genuine affection. You might think that your partner really wants to make you feel special and so he is showing you off to his friends. Unfortunately, this is not likely to be the case. Your partner wants everyone to think that *he* is special for having you as a partner. Your feelings are not important to him. Participants in our studies often report experiences like this. We have read several statements like: "I felt important when he told his friends what a popular person I was." "He would use me to show off, but I didn't mind. It actually felt pretty good." [3]

Narcissists also have their side of the story. For example, one narcissist reported that he felt really good "walking into a party with a hottie on his arm." He then suggested that this meant he was successful with women. Like most narcissists, he just did not get it. The idea that relationships may be about caring or commitment never crossed his mind.

Unfortunately, the good feeling that comes with being a trophy does not last long. The excitement wears thin. There is a growing awareness that the narcissist does not really care about you, but instead is only using you. Your feelings of "specialness" are diminished once you realize that the narcissist has dated ten other people like you and will probably date ten more. Our research participants have often described these feelings.

- "I felt like a china doll—pretty but empty."
- "It was like he had me on a leash all the time."
- "He would dote on me in public, but didn't want to spend any time alone."

It can be exciting to be used as a trophy, but it is ultimately unsatisfying.

The "trophy syndrome" just described is often a public phenomenon. The narcissist publicly displays his romantic partner and this inflates the narcissist's self-image. In private, however, there is little need for a trophy. Thus, there are other strategies that narcissists use to feel like winners. Before going into this, I need to make a brief detour into a psychological phenomenon known as the *better-than-average effect*.[4] Let me start by giving you a brief quiz:

Below is a list of personality traits. We want to know how you compare to the *average person* on each of these personality traits.

Please rate yourself relative to the *average person* on each of these personality traits using the following scale:

0 = much less than the *average person*
1 = less than the *average person*
2 = moderately less than the *average person*
3 = slightly less than the *average person*
4 = about the same as the *average person*
5 = slightly more than the *average person*
6 = moderately more than the *average person*
7 = more than the *average person*
8 = much more than the *average person*

Morality	0 1 2 3 4 ⑤ 6 7 8
Intelligence	0 1 2 3 4 ⑤ 6 7 8
Physical Attractiveness	0 1 2 3 4 ⑤ 6 7 8
Humility	0 1 2 3 ④ 5 6 7 8

If you are like most people, you probably circled a "4" or higher on each question. This is because, on average, most people, narcissists and non-narcissists alike, think that they are better than average. If this statement sounds strange, it is because it is not logically possible. If people were honest with themselves, some would think that they were better than average; some would think that they were worse than average; and some would think that they were just average. On average, people would believe that they were average.

Psychologically, however, people do believe that they are better than average. They are better than average in physical appearance, driving skills, social skills, academic skills, etc. This is something that I can reliably demonstrate in my Social Psychology class. In a typical class of thirty-five students, for example, only one or two students will say that they are below average in physical appearance. I often ask the class to rate themselves on humility. The average student almost always reports that he or she is more *humble* than the average person!

Overall, these illusions make us all feel a bit better about ourselves and they are generally harmless. There is a big exception to this better-than-average effect, however. For most people this effect will go away when the comparison is not the average person, but a close friend or dating partner. Most people will say that they are smarter, more socially skilled, and better looking than the average person, but they will *not* say that they are smarter, more socially skilled, and better looking than their close friends or dating partner.[5]

In short, people are willing to forgo their own self-promotion for the sake of the relationship. We do not go around telling our friends or dating partner that we are better than they are because: 1. If you tell your best friend that you are better looking and smarter than he or she is, your friend will be offended and perhaps no longer want to be your friend. 2. People respect and value their friends and dating partners and truly consider them to be equals in many traits. (Sometimes there are exceptions where one friend is the "smart one" and one is the "socially skilled one." In this case, the positive traits are "divided up" between the friends.) 3. When people are in close relationships, the need to constantly self-promote naturally recedes. (People do not generally interrupt conversations with their close friends to talk about how great they are.)[6]

Narcissists, however, do not follow these rules. Narcissists do not really mind offending people, including close friends. Narcissists also do not have a lot of concern for close friends. Finally, narcissists always need to promote themselves—meaningful or intimate conversations are not enough for them.

What do narcissists do instead? The narcissist uses his relationships as places to further pump up his already inflated ego. He believes that he is better than his romantic partner and will consistently rate himself smarter, better looking, and more socially-skilled than the person he is involved with, even a spouse. Basically, he is number one and you are number two.[7]

My research participants have often reported these experiences:

- "He was so competitive with me. It was like he had to win. I didn't understand it really, we were supposed to be dating and supporting each other's success."
- "Whenever I did something great at work, my boyfriend would congratulate me, but later he would seem to get kind of angry."
- "He would always put me down. He couldn't stand it if I knew more than he did."

This competition angle always seems strange to me. This is because (a) if you love someone, why wouldn't you want them to succeed, and (b) when you are in a relationship with someone, you are a team. If your partner succeeds, it is good for the team. Narcissists, however, don't like to play second fiddle. Switching metaphors, they need to be the "top dog" in the relationship. As we will see, there are other things that narcissists don't like.

I'm in Control Here

To use another example from popular culture, think of the movie *Sleeping with the Enemy*, starring Julia Roberts. In the movie, Julia's character's husband treats Julia as a trophy in public, but in private his relationship is all about control. This is illustrated pretty dramatically in the movie. For example, he demands that the cans in the kitchen be arranged a certain way and the bath towels be placed just so. Ultimately, the efforts at organization are really about controlling Julia.

This movie certainly displayed an extreme form of narcissism and control. Nevertheless, almost all narcissists insist on some element of control in their romantic relationships. This desire for control can take a variety of forms. The most extreme form involves intimidation or violence. There are also less extreme forms that rely on persuasion or emotional pressure. Finally, there are far more subtle efforts at control that rely on charm or flattery. Let's look at each of these starting with the extremes.

Narcissism may be a root cause of certain forms of relationship violence. This violence is usually triggered by a *perceived* threat to the narcissist. It is important to emphasize the word "perceived" because these threats are often not intended and may only be visible to the narcissist. An innocent comment like "Why did you choose that jacket?" could be perceived by the narcissist as an insult to his looks or style. Also, narcissists can be threatened when people leave them—even if only for a short time. For example, a woman's desire to go out with her friends may be seen as a threat by the narcissist and result in violence.

The results of these violent desires for control are, of course, highly negative for the relationship. The narcissist's girlfriend ends up walking on eggshells in order to avoid these outbursts of violence, but is only successful for short periods of time. She feels anxious and out of control, but often makes excuses for her partner. "It was my fault for criticizing him. He was under a lot of pressure."

Narcissists use other forms of control in dating relationships as well. One experience often reported by participants in my research is sexual pressure. In early stages of dating relationships, narcissists often try to pressure their partner into going further sexually than they would like. This pressure may take the form of charm with just a hint of underlying threat. It may also take the form of emotional blackmail. Narcissists will threaten to leave the relationship or to see other women if their sexual needs are not met. They may even pretend that they are hurt emotionally and try to "guilt" women into sexual actions. At the extremes, this can even involve rape—an intense display of narcissistic control. Although this is a topic big enough for a separate book, several individuals, notably Professors Baumeister and Bushman, have suggested that narcissism is implicated in many instances of rape.[8]

Narcissists also use a range of far more subtle manipulation tactics to get what they want. These are certainly more common than physical abuse. Narcissists flatter, cajole, charm, or otherwise drive their dating partners to do their bidding. One woman related to me a striking example of subtle manipulation and control. Her boyfriend would make her iron his clothes. He would not threaten her with violence or anything so overt. Instead, he would bring his laundry to her apartment and say things like, "C'mon! Think about how good I'll look in those clothes once they're ironed." Not only did he manipulate her into ironing his clothes, but he also started sneaking his friends' clothes into the pile! Eventually, she left the relationship and wondered what she had ever seen in the guy.

Another example is a woman who was planning a wedding with her (by all accounts) narcissistic fiancé. As you may know, many guys are not very involved in planning weddings. The key for many is to say, "Yeah, that looks great" and then hide. There are also some guys who make a real effort to be supportive—they want to help out, but they don't want to control the process. The narcissistic fiancé, however, was totally involved with the process because he wanted to make a great impression on the three-hundred-plus guests and thus make it one step higher on the social ladder. In fact, the fiancé was more concerned about the wedding than his bride, and would make all sorts of efforts to control the ceremony. His most outrageous move was to refuse to have one of his wife's oldest and closest friends as a bridesmaid because she was "too fat" and would "ruin the ceremony!"

What is especially dangerous about these subtle efforts at control is that when you are involved with a narcissist, you may not see them coming. Friends might say, "He's just manipulating you," or, "He's using you," but this is not always apparent when you're in the relationship (although women who get out of these relationships tend to see all the control efforts with the wisdom of hindsight).

The blindness to a narcissist's manipulation should not come as a surprise. First, a narcissist is a professional at manipulation. Most people do not spend their lives trying to control others, but narcissists do. I remember friends I had growing up who would lie all the time. Even when there was no real benefit to it, they would just lie. I couldn't tell if they were lying or not, of course, because they were so good at it. Narcissists are the same way with manipulation. They have done it their entire life and are pros.

Second, narcissists are often difficult to see through because they tell people what they want to hear. Narcissists' charm is, in part, an effort to bring you into their fantasy world. He tells you that you are special. He says that there is no one else like you. He makes you feel that everyone is admiring you. This feels good and can be so seductive that the narcissists' negative qualities are forgotten. Basically, a narcissist's charm rests on his ability to see and manipulate your own narcissistic needs.

The big picture is that a narcissist's desire for control is the same as his desire for everything else in the relationship: He wants what he wants (esteem, status, sex, whatever) and he doesn't care about you.

Empathy? Caring? Huh?

This story shows a narcissist's empathy in rare form. Tracy was dating her boyfriend Jim and the relationship was falling apart. Finally, after a big fight at her apartment, Tracy broke things off with Jim. Jim, however, decided it was too late to drive back to his place, so he decided to spend the night at Tracy's. Tracy was still crying from the emotional experience of the breakup, and Jim's comment was, "Do you mind not crying? I'm trying to sleep." Empathy? Caring? Huh?

One word that is seldom used to describe narcissists in romantic relationships is "caring." Unless, of course, the statement is "You only care about yourself." Narcissists do not display caring in relationships, nor do they display several of the behaviors that go with caring: empathy, perspective-taking, and sacrifice.

Caring implies a genuine concern for another's welfare and well-being. It often means putting the needs of the other person before the needs of oneself. It does not necessarily mean doing heroic acts for the other person. Caring can be displayed by being emotionally supportive, listening, or doing something small but nice for the person. In the studies that we have conducted, women consistently report that their narcissistic boyfriends don't do any of these things.

I was dating Jeff for about three months before I started to realize that something was wrong. When we first started dating he seemed to listen to what I said, but after a while he would totally ignore me. One night I was telling him about the lousy grade that I had received on a French test. He kept looking over my shoulder at the TV. He then said, "Let's go out to a party," I said that I didn't feel like going out. He said, "Suit yourself," and took off. The next day I was angry at him and he had no idea why.

We could be in a big discussion about something that happened to me and the next thing I know, we were talking about him. I didn't even notice it sometimes. What an ass!

These incidents occur in marriages as well. One of our research participants wrote about her husband of four years.

We were talking about spending more time together—we were even thinking about having kids. My husband did not seem interested. His comment was, "I'm really focused on

myself right now." That was not the most caring thing that I
had ever heard!

A lot of men are not that good at listening. Men are problem-focused and do much better at solving problems than talking about feelings. This doesn't mean they are uncaring, however. Men just express their caring in a more concrete way.

Narcissists are different. It isn't that he wants to be caring but don't really know how to express himself. *Narcissists do not care*. It just isn't part of his makeup. This distinction is important to draw because lots of women make excuses for narcissistic boyfriends. "He really does care about me; he just does a bad job showing it." "I know that he cares about us, but he's just really caught up at work." These excuses certainly apply to some men, but not to narcissists.

Another aspect of caring that narcissists do not display is perspective-taking. Perspective-taking is the term that psychologists use for seeing things in the relationship from the partner's point of view. Sometimes this is referred to as "standing in someone else's shoes." A great deal of relationship conflict can be avoided by stepping back and taking the point of view of the partner. What are seen as big problems often are seen as small when perspective-taking is applied.

The ability to perspective-take is difficult for many people. It involves stepping outside of your own head and seeing a different reality. Often the change in a relationship that comes from perspective-taking is dramatic.

A movie called *What Women Want* starring Mel Gibson and

Helen Hunt used a dramatic technique to demonstrate the power of perspective-taking. Mel Gibson's character was a prototypical narcissist. He was vain, egotistical, and was happy to step on others in order to meet his own needs. He had dozens of failed relationships and a daughter who barely spoke to him. One day he received an electric shock and when he awoke he had the ability to read women's thoughts. (No, this does not work, so please do not try it at home!) In essence, he was given the ultimate perspective-taking ability. At first he got nervous and wanted to get rid of the ability and go back to his egocentric reality. He then decided to use the power to exploit women, including his new boss, played by Helen Hunt. Eventually, however, this ability to perspective-take changed him and he actually became a less arrogant and selfish individual who was able to have a caring relationship with a woman.

This movie does an excellent job of portraying a narcissist who has no ability to see things from another's perspective. In the movie a strange—almost magical—event happened that forced perspective-taking on the protagonist. For narcissists in the real world, however, such magical changes do not occur. Narcissists enter relationships with no desire ever to see things from outside their own viewpoint and they do not often change. Women in our research report this all the time.

- "He never gets out of his own head."
- "Why doesn't he see things from my side once in a while?"
- "I end up bending over backwards to make him happy. He never tries to do the same for me."

One of the great benefits of being in a relationship is learning how to see the world from another's perspective and sharing your perspective on the world with someone you care about. Loving a narcissist means loving someone who will never share your world. Of course, you are always welcome to play a supporting role in his world!

There is one other important point to mention when discussing narcissists' caring: narcissists can fake it. Narcissists have the ability to feign caring and will do this at the beginning of relationships and when they want something.

Politicians often make assertions that are designed to make us think that they are good people who are only interested in relieving our suffering (think of Bill Clinton's famous line "I feel your pain"). Maybe politicians are kind and compassionate people, but there is also the possibility that they simply want our votes so they can gain political power. This is why we have all learned not to trust politicians.

Narcissists are like little politicians in the worst sense of the word. When he wants a relationship with someone, he will act caring. This caring drops off rapidly after the relationship has been established and gets boring. It is no wonder that women who date narcissists feel betrayed—the person she thought that she was dating changes into someone else. One story that I heard from a research participant captures this process.

I dated a narcissistic guy when I first started college. All my friends thought he was an egomaniac. He played on the baseball team and always talked about how popular he was. But I saw a different side of him. To me he was caring and sympathetic. I thought that I saw his true self and everyone else saw his public "superstar" side. After we had dated a few months, he started to change. He stopped calling me on week-nights and was busy all the time. He told me that he was still interested, but one day I saw him with another woman at a party. I realized then that he didn't have a hidden side—the arrogant jerk that everyone else saw was the guy I was dat-ing. I guess I was fooled into the relationship, but I seriously still think about him sometimes.

Moral: If everyone thinks that the guy that you are dating is a self-absorbed jerk, he probably is.

Can We Talk about Me for a Moment?

We all know people who somehow make every conversation about themselves. You start out talking about your day, and somehow you find yourself talking about his day:

You: I saw an interesting show on TV today. It was on French
    Cathedrals.
Him: Yeah, I saw that as well. Did you know I spent several
    months in France last year?
You: No, really?
Him: Yes, I was working on a deal over there. The French have
    a certain *joie de vivre.*

Next thing you know, you are talking about him, and the subtext of the conversation is: "Look how cool I am. I do deals and speak French."

If this example is familiar to you, you know that narcissists often reveal themselves in their conversations. Not surprisingly, they use their conversation to make themselves look and feel powerful, successful, and important. They also will display their lack of caring (unless it suits their interest to act caring and concerned). Professor Anita Vangelista and her colleagues did a fascinating series of studies on conversational narcissism[9]. They uncovered several basic strategies that narcissists use in speech:

- boasting or bragging
- refocusing the topic of conversation
- exaggerated hand movements and using a loud voice
- "glazing over"

Boasting and bragging can be very obvious. Muhammad Ali was known for saying how great he was. Today, much of the rap music that you hear is filled with flagrant boasting. Anytime someone says, "I am the best" or "I am smarter than everyone else," that is boasting.

More subtle forms of boasting and bragging also exist, however, and these are the ones that are often more effective. The example above is filled with subtle boasting: I have been to France. I am important enough to do deals over there. I speak the language because I am smart and sophisticated. These boasts just get worked into the topic of the conversation.

One of narcissists' favorite tricks is to name-drop, because that shows they are associated with powerful and important people. Another trick is to talk about places they have been. I was sitting next to a woman at a meal a few months ago who spent the entire time listing all the restaurants that she had visited on her trip to the area, and naming all the fancy wines that she had consumed. Her goal was not to share her enthusiasm for braised lamb or Chilean wine. Her goal was to impress me (and herself) with her sophistication.

Another related trick narcissists use is simple "one-upmanship." In less polite company this is known as getting into a pissing contest with someone. The basic strategy is to outdo everything that the other person in the conversation says.

You: I am excited about my bonus this year; I am almost making a six-figure salary.
Him: Yeah, I started out making six figures a few years back.

This conversational style can be pretty annoying, but it serves the narcissist's purpose, which is staying on top.

Another related trick that narcissists use is to refocus the topic of conversation from you to themselves. The example I gave at the beginning of this section was an example of this technique. To do this effectively, you need to subtly redirect the conversation onto you. If you are subtle enough, the person you are talking to doesn't even notice. In fact, they might even think that you are being supportive by talking to them. Communication scientists call this a "shift response" because the course of the conversation is shifted.

Narcissists who are really good won't do this all the time. Sometimes, they will be supportive for a little while, but next thing you know, the conversation has turned back to them.

You: I had a run-in with my boss today.
Him: That must have been tough.
You: Yeah, it was. He can be a real jerk.
Him: Yeah, I know how that is. When I was managing the marketing department I had several tough conversations with employees.
You: What was that like?

Just like that, the conversation has shifted from you to him. And the best part is that you still think that he cares about your issues. Pretty clever on the narcissist's part!

Not only does the narcissist use the topic of conversation to enhance himself, but he also uses a particular style of conversation. One strategy for both drawing attention to himself and for dominating a conversation is showing exaggerated hand movements, and also a loud and dominating voice. This does not necessarily mean yelling. Instead, it can mean talking in a forceful but controlled manner. Even the whole body can be used to show dominance. Researchers have found that narcissists display pride by puffing out their chests and putting their hands on their sides—sort of like an evil superman. These power gestures often make others assume more submissive poses.[10]

A final conversational technique used by narcissists is a "glazed over" look. They do this when they simply want to express an absolute lack of concern with you and your life. This may be accompanied by utterances like, "Huh, what was that?" This glazed look also shows how powerful the narcissist is. Think about it. If you are talking to your boss, you pay attention. Your boss, on the other hand, may glaze over when you talk to him. He's the boss—he doesn't have to care. A narcissist may not be your boss, but he will think that he is. And he doesn't care. Thus, the glazed-over look works.

In closing, let me stress that the techniques narcissists use in conversations can be very subtle. The people that a narcissist is talking to often don't even know what has happened. I have even had people tell me that he or she knew someone for years before they realized that he was using all these techniques. Remember, narcissists spend their lives striving to have power and control over people—and to look good doing it! Don't blame yourself if you get sucked in.

Wandering Eyes (or, What You Don't Know Won't Hurt You)

There is a great old Joni Mitchell song called "Coyote." The song uses the metaphor of the coyote to describe a desirable man who is always pursuing some woman or another. He is always looking for something new to chase. He sees a pair of pretty legs and he is off and running. Narcissists may approach women like coyotes approach rabbits: He sees a woman and the impulse is to start chasing.

This finding is observed again and again in our research. Narcissists report elevated scores on what psychologists call *attention to relationship alternatives*. This scale, developed by Professor Rowland Miller of Sam Houston State University, measures the extent to which individuals in relationships flirt with members of the opposite sex and go out with other people without telling their romantic partner. We often find a pattern in dating couples where the narcissistic boyfriend reports seeing other women and his girlfriend has no idea what is going on. Indeed, she is only focused on him and the relationship.[11]

Below are a couple of the items from the Attention to Alternatives scale:

- I am distracted by people whom I find attractive.
- I go out socially with opposite sex friends without telling my partner.

There are several reasons for narcissists' "wandering eyes" in relationships. For one thing, narcissists think that they are wonderful and attractive to members of the opposite sex. Narcissists live in a fantasy world where all sorts of women want to date them, so, hey, why not give it a try? People use various phrases to describe narcissists in romantic relationships. One is "God's gift to women," as in: "He thinks that he is God's gift to women." This phrase captures precisely the narcissist's belief about his social world. Narcissists think that women desire them and they are surrounded by temptation.

Narcissists are also always on the search for "a better deal." They maintain relationships in part to meet self-esteem needs. They want that certain "trophy" partner that will let the world know that they are winners. The problem with trophies is that there is always a better one out there. The narcissist just needs to keep looking.

If you look at things from the narcissist's perspective, women, at best, are like cars. You might find someone who is a BMW. It looks great and you feel pretty good driving around in front of your friends. But let's say you start to see this great-looking Porsche in your neighborhood. Pretty soon the BMW is forgotten and getting that Porsche is seen as the real ticket to success. Soon, however, even the Porsche becomes less desirable when the new model Porsche makes an appearance. The narcissist then spends his energy trying to be the first guy on the block to own the newest Porsche. And on and on and on.... To give an example of this, a friend was dating a guy in high school who enjoyed using the quaint expression, "I'd do her," whenever he'd see an attractive woman. And this was when he was hanging around with his girlfriend. When she called him on it, he retorted with unassailable logic: "Hey, I've got a car, but that doesn't mean I can't admire other cars."

This certainly sounds cold. In fact, it *is* cold. Unfortunately, this is the way that many narcissists approach a romantic relationship. The narcissist is always attuned to the possibilities out there for a better-looking, more exotic, or more popular partner. Participants in our research have told this story over and over.

- "He stopped calling and next thing I knew he was dating another woman I work with."
- "He left me for a dancer."
- "He cheated on me with my best friend."

What is really destructive about narcissists is not that they find other romantic partners. What is really destructive is that (a) narcissists seek out other partners when they are already in a supposedly committed romantic relationship and (b) narcissists lie about it without hesitation. They definitely do some damage to women's trust in men.

It is clear that narcissists think that they are God's gift to women and are always on the lookout for a better partner. To make matters worse, narcissists get a kick out of the whole process—even when they hurt others. Narcissists are high in what psychologists call *sensation seeking*. That is, they crave excitement and novel experiences. They don't focus on getting caught. Rather, narcissists focus on how great they will feel when they can pull it off. Sneaking behind their girlfriend's back, sweet-talking new women, and lying to all concerned is exciting. It's challenging and arousing and thus enjoyable for the narcissist.[12]

Students in my psychology classes often ask what I think about President Clinton's affair with Monica Lewinsky. Based on the details I have read in the press, I always imagined that the affair was, among other things, just plain exciting for the President. It could be that he was revved up by the idea of carrying on with a young intern in the Oval Office while a foreign leader was on the phone. The risk and "wrongness" of the affair may have made it particularly titillating.

I do not think that he (or even narcissists) deliberately set out to hurt other people, although this is almost always the result of their behavior. I think that it is more precise to say that narcissists do not take others' feelings into consideration. They just don't care about others the same way that they care about themselves. In the end, narcissists do whatever they want and whatever they think they can get away with.

One clear example of this is what psychologists call *mate poaching*.[13] Mate poaching is the effort to steal someone else's partner away from them. This is really destructive behavior because it ruins a relationship, but it happens all the time. Narcissists, in particular, are willing to steal other people's partners. Of course, these relationships that are the result of mate poaching don't last that long. If someone steals you, he is probably going to steal someone else.[14]

Narcissists also gain an additional, "fringe" benefit from their wandering eyes. This benefit is somewhat subtle and I will attempt to explain it in a bit of a roundabout way. Imagine that you want a new car. You tell the salesperson that you really, really, really love the car, but you want a good price for it. Now imagine that you are the salesperson. Are you going to give in and offer a low price for the car? Or, are you going to think, "I've got her," and offer only a high price for the car? Most salespeople in this situation will use the latter strategy. He or she will recognize an advantage over the buyer and try to get as much money as possible.

Now imagine that you use a different strategy with the car dealer. You say that you are a little bit interested in the car, but there is another car at a different dealer that appeals to you as well. When the salesperson hears this, what will he do? Chances are, if he believes you, he will offer you a discounted price on the car in order to keep your interest. The moral of this car shopping story is that the person with the least to gain from the transaction has the greater power. The buyer that appears *less* interested in the car will get the *better* deal.

Not surprisingly, this same principle applies to the marketplace of romantic relationships. The person in the relationship who is less interested will have more power. Psychologists call this the *principle of least interest.*

How could this principle work in narcissists' favor? As we have said earlier, narcissists crave power in their relationships. One way of getting this power is to be the less interested member in the relationships. Narcissists are able to maintain this lack of interest by having alternative dating partners.

Let me clarify this with an example: Jeff and Jody are dating. Jody thinks Jeff is terrific and can't imagine being with any other man. Jeff, on the other hand, has lots of women who he is interested in dating. He does like Jody, but he also likes Jennifer, Julie, and Jasmine. Basically, Jeff has many more potential dating partners than Jody does. This weekend Jody really wants to go to the movies and see the latest romantic comedy. Jeff wants to go out to a party with some of his old college friends. Who would you guess would have his or her way in this conflict? It is clear that Jeff has the power in the relationship—if Jody doesn't do what he wants, he really wouldn't care all that much. Thus, Jody and Jeff end up going to the party. A narcissist's wandering eyes give him more power over his girlfriend.[15]

In sum, a narcissist will flirt with potential dating partners even when he currently is in a relationship. There are reasons for this. The narcissist thinks that he is highly attractive and thus assumes that many women will be open to his advances. The narcissist also is on the lookout for a better-looking or more popular partner—he wants the best trophy that he can find. Likewise, the narcissist gets a thrill out of running around. It's like an exciting game to them. Finally, the narcissist is able to maintain power in his relationship by keeping a string of replacement partners on the horizon. As long as he is the less interested party in the relationship, he will have all the power. As we will see in the next section, none of this bodes well for narcissist's commitment to a relationship.

Commitment is Great—for Other People (or, "The List")

I heard this story from a former student. Mia was dating Wayne, and was deeply in love with him. Wayne was charming and a lot of fun at parties—except that he had a bit of a tendency to over-drink.

He was a fairly good-looking guy, but thought that he was better looking than he actually was. He was athletic and had played hockey in college. He also seemed to be smart and successful.

They dated for over a year and had few apparent problems. They weren't necessarily talking marriage, but Wayne had told Mia that he loved her (as she noted, not only when he was drunk, although he was drunk quite a bit). The big problem came when Mia met Andi. Wayne introduced Andi to Mia as one of his girl "friends." Mia and Andi soon became friends, and Andi confessed that she had been more than a friend to Wayne in the recent past. Mia confronted Wayne about this, and he said his relationship with Andi didn't mean anything, and, besides, it was all in the past.

Mia wasn't entirely convinced by Wayne, but gave him the benefit of the doubt. Then, on New Year's Eve they were supposed to go out with Mia's family. While Wayne was in the shower, Mia casually picked up a book that she had given him for a Christmas gift. Inside the book she found a list of every woman that Wayne had slept with. There were eighty-nine names on the list. Mia was number fifty-nine and Andi was number forty. Beside each of the names (except for hers and Andi's) there was a brief description. Wayne was using mnemonic devices so that he could remember each sexual conquest! These descriptions included pleasant things like "Pig," "Double-teamed in club," and "screwed in Club XT."

Mia confronted Wayne about the list. Wayne used the classic narcissistic excuse: It didn't mean anything. Then, he blamed Mia for snooping in his private affairs. He also explained that he had never really made a commitment to Mia, and that the year and a half that they spent together and all the times he said that he loved her really didn't imply a commitment.

Eventually, however, Mia got the whole story. Wayne was having a competition with a friend to see how many women they could sleep with. It also turned out that Wayne had a secret double-life going to clubs where ecstasy was frequently used. Mia was smart enough to leave the relationship, but she had her heart broken and spent the next several months thinking about Wayne.

Wayne was a classic narcissist. He viewed romantic relationships as a way of gaining power, status, and excitement. He didn't care about his partner's feelings. What really struck me about this story was that Wayne was willing to really hurt his girlfriend (as well as who knows how many other women) in order to win a competition with a friend. It was all about ego.

This story also illustrates a destructive formula for narcissists' relationships—many alternatives lead to less commitment. In order to elaborate on this point, I will need to take yet another detour into some basic psychological theory about romantic relationships.

Researcher Caryl Rusbult has spent her career at the University of North Carolina studying the factors that drive commitment in romantic relationships. Surprisingly, these factors can be placed into only three categories. The first is *satisfaction*. People will stay in relationships to the extent that he or she is satisfied. For example, he finds his partner attractive, they have fun together, and are emotionally supportive of each other. Basically, when rewards are greater than costs, people will be satisfied. The second factor is *investments*. This is something that most people do not think of, but has a powerful effect on commitment. *Investments* include such things as time, shared friends, a shared house or apartment, or shared finances. What is striking to me is that lots of people will stay committed to unsatisfying relationships because they have "put lots of time into it." This doesn't make much sense rationally, but it is a powerful force in relationships. The third factor that leads to commitment is *alternative dating partners*. More precisely, to the extent that an individual does *not* have alternatives to the relationships, she or he will stay committed. If you think there are lots of others out there to date, you will be less committed; if you think there are few others out there to date, you will be more committed. Hence the insult: "Even if you were the last man I earth I would not go out with you."[16]

Now that we know the factors that lead to commitment, where does narcissism fit in? It is really pretty straightforward. Narcissists have many alternative dating partners; therefore, they are less committed to their romantic relationships. [17]

In the previous example, Wayne was dating a terrific woman, Mia. Wayne, however, had dozens of alternative dating partners available, and thus his commitment to his relationship with Mia was minimal. This is what we find with most of the narcissists in our studies. The narcissist reports that he has a large number of potential dating partners and consequently reports little commitment to his current dating relationship.

There is no doubt that commitment is important to relationships. The greater the commitment, the longer that relationships will endure. People generally remain in a relationship as long as they are committed. When commitment drops, relationships often end.

Commitment also has a pervasive impact on the *quality* of the relationship. To the extent that an individual is committed to a relationship he or she will do things to keep the relationship going. Think about it, when you buy a new house, you may love it the way it is, but you fully expect that you will have to do lots of maintenance work to keep it that way. You have to mow the lawn, repaint, fix leaky faucets, and change the air filters. You also have to avoid damaging it. For example, you can't throw things at the walls or eat on the carpet.

For some reason, however, most people think that relationships, unlike everything else in life, don't need maintenance work. This isn't the case—relationships need to be cared for and maintained. Dr. Rusbult has referred to these strategies for maintaining relationships as *relationship maintenance mechanisms*. Some of these are behavioral. For example, committed people are willing to sacrifice his or her own desires for the good of the relationship. My wife was willing to move from lovely Chapel Hill, North Carolina, to Cleveland with me (no offense to the good people of Cleveland!) so that I could pursue my post-doctoral education.

Other relationship maintenance mechanisms are psychological. For example, when people are in committed relationships, they tend to use the pronoun "we" rather than "I" when describing a relationship. In their minds, they view themselves as one unit. [18]

Probably the most important of these mechanisms is *accommodation*—the tendency to respond constructively to destructive behaviors on the part of the partner. This is a somewhat technical way of saying: be nice even when your partner does something nasty.[19] Let me give an example. Kathleen and Rob are living together. Rob comes home after a long day at work. Kathleen says, "Welcome back," and Rob says, "Leave me alone—I need some space." Kathleen has a couple of choices at this point. She can do something positive in response—for example, ask Rob why he is in a foul mood or wait a few minutes for him to settle down. Likewise, she can do something negative in response—for example, tell Rob that he is a total jerk or storm out of the house.

If Kathleen responds positively, Rob is likely to apologize eventually and a real fight will be avoided. On the other hand, if Kathleen responds negatively, Rob is likely to fire back with a negative response. Kathleen will then get even nastier and eventually things might get really destructive. "I hate you." "You are always an ass." "I can't stand you." It's tough to take these kinds of statements back. In fact, some psychologists have argued that it actually takes five positive events to make up for one negative event.[20] Even an expensive diamond ring isn't enough to make up for some things.

Everyone acts like a jerk at one time or another in a relationship. Relationships work best when both partners respond to these nasty behaviors in a positive way. This doesn't mean being a door-mat. Instead, it means standing up for yourself in a way that solves the problem rather than exacerbates it.

One of the problems with dating narcissists is that to the extent that he is not committed to the relationship, he will not be accommodating in the relationship. Narcissists will respond to your bad behaviors by being nasty or leaving. That means that there is likely to be more fighting and conflict. When narcissists stay they can make the relationship—and you—really miserable. There will be high drama and many ups and downs.

There is a final point that I would like to address regarding narcissists and commitment. There is little doubt that narcissists show a lack of commitment in their dating life. My viewpoint is that narcissists are basically selfish. They want relationships with lots of women, in part because it makes them look cool, feel popular and important, and in part because it is fun. This, in and of itself, is fine—if both partners are aware of the rules. The problem is that narcissists keep this attitude when they are in supposedly committed relationships. Narcissists may be fun for a spring break fling, but they are lousy people with whom to attempt to have a caring or committed relationship.

There is another school of thought, however, that sees narcissists as people who actually want commitment but are scared of it at some unconscious level. These therapists claim that narcissists have experienced rejection at a young age and that their fear of intimacy as adults is a result. We should feel compassion for narcissists because they are deeply troubled. We should also help them with love and therapy.

My opinion is that this latter theory regarding narcissists' lack of commitment probably holds up for only a very small minority of narcissists (if that). Furthermore, I think that it's a dangerous belief to have when you fall in love with a narcissist. You might think that he can be cured of his infidelity and selfishness if he only feels that he can trust in your love. I have not found any evidence at all of this happening in any research literature. Over and over again, I have heard about women being hurt by narcissists and narcissists not feeling all that bad about it.

Surprisingly (or not, depending on your perspective), two of our graduate students have recently found evidence that narcissists actually become *more* unfaithful when they think that their partners are committed to them. In the study, narcissists and non-narcissists listed all the reasons that they knew their partner was committed to them. When the non-narcissists wrote about a partner's high level of commitment to the relationships, they reported *less* interest in dating other people. This makes sense—if your partner loves you, why would you want to leave? When narcissists thought that a partner was committed, however, they were actually *more* willing to cheat on their partner. This makes sense from the narcissists' perspective. If my partner is highly committed, then I can cheat and get away with it. What a great deal for me![21]

Bottom line: Guys who are narcissistic jerks on the outside are likely to be narcissistic jerks on the inside. Furthermore, they *like* being narcissistic jerks. It makes them happy.

What do Narcissists Call Love?

Whenever I teach a class on love, I start by asking the students how many of them know what love is. Most will raise their hands. I then ask them what love is. Someone will usually say that love is caring. Somebody else will say love is about sexual chemistry. Someone will then counter that chemistry is lust. One student will usually say that there is a difference between being "in love" and loving someone. After twenty minutes of this, I will usually have written thirty things on the board and the class will not have agreed on what love really is. The message of the exercise is that love is a funny thing. We all think that we know what it is, we all talk about it, but we often disagree on the correct definition.

Scientific psychologists have not spent much energy trying to find the true nature of love. Rather, they have tried to understand how normal people *think about* love. One popular approach championed by psychologist Robert Sternberg at Yale has found that love has three distinct components. The first of these is *passion* or a physical/emotional attraction to the other person. The second component is *intimacy* or shared personal knowledge with another person. The final component is *commitment* or the desire to maintain a relationship with the other person.[22]

Most of the time when people think of love, especially when it refers to a "healthy" relationship, they are thinking of one or a combination of these three components. For example, you hear people say that someone is their lover and best friend. This reflects both the passion and intimacy components of love. Likewise, people often think of elderly married couples as having love that includes a great deal of friendship and intimacy.

There are other experiences of love as well. These emerge particularly in "unhealthy" relationships. Research by Clyde and Susan Hendrick at Texas Tech have measured six aspects of love that tap into both its healthy and unhealthy components. These researchers examine six love styles: *erotic*, *game playing*, *companionate*, *pragmatic*, *lovesick*, and *selfless*. Several of these map onto the three characteristics I just described. For example, erotic love is essentially equivalent to passion. Companionate love has to do with being close friends with the person you love and is a lot like intimacy.[23]

The other love styles are a little different. Game-playing love is really the approach taken by "players." They see love as a game and enjoy keeping their partner uncertain about their commitment while at the same time seeing other partners on the side. Pragmatic love has to do with finding Mr. or Mrs. Right—a person that your family or friends will approve of. Love sickness refers to several of the physical experiences of love: butterflies in the stomach, an inability to sleep, and extreme feelings of depression and elation. (Yes, some people think that it is not love unless you want to throw-up when you see the person.) Finally, selflessness refers to empathy or compassion for the other person. It is the knowledge that you would do almost anything for the other person that reveals your love.

In short, researchers have found that people can experience love in many different ways. Some people think they are in love when they feel compassion for another person; others need to get sick to their stomach. Some know that it is love when they find a person who meets their image of what will be perfect for their life; others think that love is all about sexual passion. In order to understand narcissists, it is important to know that love can have different meanings to different people.

So, how do narcissists experience love?[24] We should first discuss what narcissists are not. They are not selfless. They do not want to put the needs of romantic partners before their own needs. Even in love relationships narcissists look out for number one. This should not come as a surprise after our long discussion of narcissists, but it does often come as a surprise to those who are dating narcissists.

When you are in a romantic relationship with someone, there is an implicit understanding that your partner will not only look out for your interests, but also on occasion put your interests before his own. These selfless acts are not the dramatic ones that we see in the movies where someone gives up his life for his lover. Rather, they are the smaller unselfish actions that really add up in a relationship. For example, if you are flying into the airport late at night after a business trip, your partner might not want to drive into the city to pick you up, but he will make the drive to the extent that being selfless is important to his experience of relationships.

Narcissists do not have this view of relationships. He is likely to say, "take a cab" unless there is something in it for them. A story that I heard from one of my students really brought this home.

Jean was asked by her new boyfriend, Mike, to go to a fraternity formal. This sounded like it would be a nice weekend for Jean, so she said yes. Mike was at a different school so she had to take a flight to meet him. Mike did not offer to pay for the ticket, but Jean went anyway thinking that perhaps it was an oversight. When she landed, Mike was not at the airport as he had promised. Instead, he sent a pledge from the fraternity to meet her at the airport and drive her to his fraternity. When Jean arrived, she had to wait for an hour before Mike showed up. His excuse was that something came up. When he finally did arrive, he brought her up to his room but did not offer to carry her bag. At this point, Jean started to get the idea that this might not be the best weekend.

Things got better as they got ready for the party. He was charming and he did make a big show of escorting Jean into the room where the prom was and introducing her to his friends. Soon, however, Mike was drinking a little too much and excused himself. Jean waited alone for a while and then went to look for him. Mike was hanging out with some friends doing "shots" by the bathroom and laughing, when he saw Jean he shrugged his shoulders and then told her to "hang out" because he had to leave for a minute. An hour later he had not returned to the party. Jean ended up sharing a ride back to the fraternity where she waited. Mike had not shown up by ten the next morning so Jean got a cab to the airport and left. When she spoke to Mike the next day, he was perplexed and a bit angry that she had left. He thought that she was lucky to have gone to the formal with him and—hey— what did she expect from him anyway?

Narcissists are selfish in love. Furthermore, they are not totally aware of the impact that their selfishness has on others. This is not a positive ingredient for a long-term relationship.

Now that we know how narcissists do not approach love, we can tackle the problem of *how* narcissists do experience love. The best descriptor of narcissists' love style is game playing. We have found this over and over in our research. Narcissists are "players" in their romantic relationships. They flirt with other people, they lie to partners about dating other people, and they get kick out of keeping their partner uncertain about their level of commitment. One day it is "I love you," the next it is a total brush off.

I have heard so many stories about narcissists' game playing that it is difficult to pick one out to use as an example. Narcissists come on as smooth and confident, they are charming and talkative, and they can be fun to date for a while. They thrive in the initial stages of a relationship. They are so good at this that they want to experience these initial relationship stages with different women at the same time. When issues of commitment come up narcissists are not very agreeable, but they are good at stringing along their partners for extended periods. Here is one story from a friend:

Marcy was a successful marketing executive in a large Southern city. She met Gene, a management consultant, at a company party. She felt immediately attracted to Gene when they met. He was dressed in a leather coat that set him apart from the other guests at the party. He walked across the room to where she was sitting with a friend and introduced himself. They talked quite a bit and, before the party was over, they had made plans to go out the next weekend. The first date was fantastic. Gene knew several people at the restaurant where they ate and Marcy felt that he was part of the "in crowd." Their relationship started at that point and soon Marcy started having thoughts that Gene might be "Mr. Right." Unfortunately, she noted some problems in the relationship. Gene often would not return her calls. Also, Marcy's friends did not seem to be as taken with Gene as she was. Finally, whenever the topic of commitment would come up, Gene would smile and change the subject.

The more Marcy tried to get close to Gene, the more Gene would pull away. Business trips would come up again and again, and he did not want to go out as often as she wanted to. The last straw was that Marcy found out that Gene had asked out another woman from her company while they were dating. She confronted Gene and he did not appear riddled with guilt. Instead he said, "Look, we're not married. What do you want?" She spent another three months in the relationship trying to get him to commit, but eventually gave up.

Gene was a classic narcissist game player. Marcy knew there was something wrong at some level, but, as with many women (and men, for that matter), it took a lot for her to leave the relationship. It is also important to note that Gene (and narcissists in general) know that they are players. They like to be players. It makes them feel powerful and free. The power comes from the principle of least interest described earlier. It is also fun for them.

As I mentioned in the last section, *I do not believe that narcissists have any loving, kind person "deep inside."* I do not believe that narcissists hate themselves for being cads and secretly want to be in stable, loving relationships. Narcissists are just in it for fun, ego, and power.

I want to end this section with a quick mention of an idea that I see time and again in the "self-help" literature. This is the idea that *someone must love themselves before they can love others.* People hear this and they think that the secret to good relationships is to have a high self-opinion. The problem with this statement is that it is half right, and half very wrong. Narcissists are the people in our society who really love themselves and they have little desire or ability to love others. Does this mean that self-loathing is the key to true love? Far from it. Self-loathing and depression are bad for relationships. The best recipe for loving others seems to be a combination of *low* narcissism and *high* self-esteem. Relationships are enhanced by having a healthy self-esteem and at the same time a positive opinion of one's partner. Narcissistic self-love is not the answer.

Bling Bling: Narcissism and Materialism

I was stopped at a gas station a few weeks back when some guy drove in with his music blaring. He was in a purple custom-painted pick-up. It was so low to the ground that a speed bump would rip off the transmission and the windows were so tinted that I couldn't actually see him. He had those flashy chrome rims that I see all the time now. I imagine that they cost a month's pay. There were neon lights coming out of the bottom of the truck so it looked a bit like a space craft.

Being a psychologist, my first thought was to wonder what kind of person would drive a car like that? So, I asked myself: What social purpose would such a car serve? What kind of message would it send out and who would be the ideal target of that message? (Often, when you are not the target of something, it is difficult to understand. When I talk to advertising and marketing people, for example, they always say that if you don't like a commercial on TV, you were probably not the intended audience.)

So, how would I interpret the message of the cheesy truck? Well, the first thing I realized was that I had paid attention to the truck. There were probably ten other cars in the parking lot, but I was looking at and thinking about the stupid truck. Between the neon lights, garish paint, and loud music, the truck had grabbed my attention. So, I thought that gaining attention was one goal of the truck.

Second, I decided that there were a lot of ways of gaining attention. The driver could have, for example, driven in a noisy, broken down truck covered with baby dolls (I have seen a few of these over the years). However, the driver had a shiny truck with an expensive paint job and expensive chrome rims. Therefore, the second part of the message was status or wealth. The truck driver is saying: Look at me! I am important and wealthy!

Third, the truck was a run-of-the-mill truck that had been customized. The standard paint and tires weren't enough for the owner. He needed something different—something that would make him stand out from the crowd. The third message of the tacky truck was: I am unique and special—not like all those other trucks!

Finally, and this is more subtle (unlike the truck!), I thought about the truck in terms of the target audience. Who is the driver trying to impress with his status and specialness? My guess was that I wasn't the intended target; I would have been impressed by a restored Porsche Spider. Instead, it was probably young and relatively immature women who were potentially interested in having a fling (more on this in a second). Stable and secure guys in long-term relationships don't have neon lights. I drive a station wagon. The license plate is not CHIKWGN.

So, the guy in the truck may have been a lot smarter than he first appeared. He was driving around a message that said: I am wealthy; I have status; I am one-of-a-kind; check me out, ladies! This is probably not the most effective message, but I figured he, like most narcissists, was playing a numbers game. He cruises down a hundred streets with ten women each, and he will find some takers.

Now, the truck with the chrome rims might seem goofy to many people, but the same type of materialism can be seen in various and more understated forms all over the place. These include expensive Italian suits, Swiss watches, and boots of Spanish leather. The key to all these things, however, is the purpose. If the purpose is to simply to draw attention to the self and convey status, wealth, and uniqueness, you are talking about narcissistic materialism.

What is wrong with materialism? Does materialism interfere with committed relationships? The answer appears to be "Yes." When I first started studying relationships with narcissists, women reported again and again that materialism was one of the biggest problems in dating narcissistic men. This was surprising to me at first. I hadn't thought of materialism in relationships before, but the more I researched the topic, the clearer it became.

What is it that makes materialism such a problem? First, I think it is because there is a willingness to substitute things for people. Narcissists often put things on an equal level with people; whereas, for most of us, things are not a reasonable substitute for people. Let me start by describing someone in a caring relationship.

Imagine that Bobby is in a caring, long-term relationship with Naomi. Naomi is out of the country for a month and Bobby misses her. For Bobby, a car or suit won't fill the gap caused by his missing partner. The only materials that may help are reminders of Naomi herself. These might be pictures, a favorite object, or eating food that he knows Naomi loves. In this case, things are used to bring the relationship to mind. This is why you always see people grab the photographs when their homes burn down, even though the photos have little material value.

Imagine that Rob the narcissist is in a long-term relationship with Nagela. Nagela is out of the country for the month and Rob misses having her around. What Rob is missing is not caring and intimacy. He is missing the status and esteem he gets from his relationship with Nagela. The good news for Rob is that he can simply replace this missing esteem with material goods. For example, if Rob was feeling down, he could throw on an expensive suit or go test drive a German sports car. Psychologically, these material possessions would do many of the same things for him that his girlfriend would.

Finally, imagine that you were dating Bobby or Rob. If you left town and knew that Bobby put a picture of you on his desk, you would probably feel pretty good. This would not interfere with the relationship in any way. It would probably enhance it. However, if you were dating Rob and realized that you were replaced by his true love, a BMW, you would be pretty upset.

Second, a related issue is one of priorities. This is pretty straightforward. If you are dating a guy who spends all his time on stuff, there will be little time left over for you. There is only so much time in the day and people only have so much mental capacity. If too much of that time and space is spent pursuing material goods, there will be little left over for caring relationships.

Narcissists can sometimes be identified when you first meet them because this is when they are most likely to talk about possessions—especially those that convey status and power. He may mention a fancy car that he has, or a summerhouse, or a plasma screen TV. (The fact that these things are leased will probably not be mentioned.) He may talk about expensive food or drinks, or, if you are out, order a drink that conveys status. There is even the observation in the clinical literature that when narcissists use drugs they use high-status drugs! A narcissist might use cocaine (high status) but not use crack (same drug, but less status).[25]

I have done some research on materialism with Dr. Kathleen Vohs, who is a marketing professor. We set up a situation where individuals were told that he or she was going to meet a stranger and talk about several topics. We gave them a list of topics to choose from with things like hobbies and more emotional topics. What the narcissists wanted to talk about was material possessions—and they really wanted to talk about their possessions more when the person they were going to talk to was someone of the opposite sex. Basically, a narcissist saw his conversation as an opportunity to show off to the other person and to gain her admiration.

There is more to materialism than just talking about it, however. Displaying wealth can serve as a signal to potential mates. "Bling bling" is the most flagrant example of this. One of my students told me that "bling" refers to anything shiny, such as diamond jewelry. The term supposedly represents the sound that light makes flashing off of a diamond or similar jewel. B-L-I-N-G. I saw a rap video where a guy had a huge medallion around his neck that would spin and flash. That seemed the epitome of "bling bling" to me.

From my perspective as a fashion critic, this type of jewelry seems utterly tacky. As a psychologist, however, I think it is a wonderful example of materialism in action. To explain this, I need to take a brief detour into the evolutionary psychology of long- and short-term relationships.[26]

According to evolutionary psychologists, relationships involve some basic exchange. The biggest difference between the sexes is in the areas of fertility and resources. Women bring fertility (usually in the forms of attractive looks and youth); men bring resources. Individuals sometimes take offense to this idea, but he or she still uses it to explain why Anna Nicole Smith married a really rich old guy.

It is more complicated than this, however, in that women and men both are built to have long-term and short-term relationships. Men do this more frequently, but women do it quite often. What do I mean by short and long term? Short-term relationships are one-night stands, brief affairs, romantic weekends, or summer flings. Long-term relationships today usually have lifetime marriage as a possibility, if not the ideal.

Now, imagine that you are a guy looking for a short-term relationship. Your goal is to find a woman who will have a short-term relationship with you. This is a tough assignment as women generally are not interested. So, you have to know who to target and how to target them. Women, on the other hand, have an easier job, as many men are interested in short-term relationships. This point is illustrated in a wonderful study conducted by Drs. Clark and Hatfield. The study itself was very simple. Two attractive experimenters, one male and one female, stood out on campus and asked total strangers one of three questions. Would you have dinner with me? Would you come back to my apartment? Would you have sex with me? The results were clear as can be. In response to the date question, roughly 45 percent of women and 55 percent of men answered "yes." Those numbers changed dramatically in response to the apartment question, where roughly 65 percent of men, but only 5 percent of women said "yes." Finally, the greatest difference was found on the sex condition, where none of the women said "yes," but roughly 70 percent of men did. Men were more willing to have sex with a complete stranger than they were to have dinner with her! The moral of this story, of course, is that it is not difficult to get someone to sleep with you if you are a woman, but it takes much more than a simple question if you are a man.[27]

So, a man seeking women for short-term relationships need to find those women who are interested. He also needs to know what these women want. According to evolutionary theory, women are looking for resources. In a long-term relationship, money and jewels are not so important. Instead, what is important is *potential*. A man who is ambitious and in medical school will be attractive for a long-term relationship even if he is 100,000 dollars in debt. He will be less attractive for a short-term relationship because potential does not cut it in short-term relationships. Instead, what matters is actual resources that—and here is the key—can be extracted quickly from the man. A woman will be more likely to have a short-term relationship with a man if she can get something out of it right away. Prostitution is the extreme example of this, but there are many more discrete forms out there.

This is where "bling bling" comes in. A flashy display of material things signals that a man has wealth. What's more, the utter foolishness of the display suggests that a man is willing to share his wealth quickly. Imagine two guys at a bar: Fred, the "player," is wearing an expensive Italian suit, a diamond encrusted Rolex watch, a large gold chain, and a diamond stud in his ear. He sits in a booth and orders a bottle of expensive French champagne. He pays the waiter with cash, which he carries in a roll in his pocket. He publicly tips the waiter with a twenty and puts on a confident smile. What is Fred's message? Is he saying, "I am a nice guy looking for a committed relationship with just the right women?" Not really. He is saying, "Check me out. If you are looking for a good time, I am your guy. I am where the action is and I am not afraid to spend some money on you." In short, Fred is hitting all the evolutionary buttons for a short-term relationship.

Mike, on the other hand, is sitting at the bar with some friends. He is drinking a beer (whatever is on tap) and talking. He is dressed in some khaki pants and a white shirt—pretty standard stuff. He is not shy, but he doesn't have a neon sign over his head saying, "for a good time call Mike." Mike is probably going to go home with the same friends he came to the bar with, but if you are looking for a committed relationship, Mike is more likely to be your guy.

This is part of what makes narcissists so tricky. Fred may look cheesy, but the bottom line is that he is the one at the bar getting the attention. It looks like it would be a lot more fun to get caught up in Fred's exciting universe than to hang out with Mike.

Of course, "bling bling" is the extreme of shallow displays of wealth. There are more tactful ways that this can be accomplished: a stainless steel Rolex watch without the diamonds, a platinum American Express card instead of the roll of bills, a silk shirt instead of the Italian suit. A narcissists markets himself for his target audience, and he adjusts his materialistic displays accordingly.

Manipulative Weasels—Emotion and Deception

We have all witnessed the scene where some narcissistic guy is trying to get back with his girlfriend after cheating, lying, or vanishing (take your pick). He puts on a smarmy smile, professes his undying love (which he discovered only after sleeping with her best friend) and then tears well up in his eyes. His girlfriend, of course, resists at first, but then buys the act and reaffirms the relationship.

What is amazing is that everyone watching this scene knows that the guy is lying through his teeth. We start using the s-words (slime, snake, sleaze). The only person who appears to buy the story is the girlfriend. She thinks that the tears and declarations of love reflect real emotion on the part of the narcissist.

Why does this act work? First, narcissists can be consummate actors. They have spent a lifetime practicing manipulating people and this has worked for them. They possess the charm and charisma that allows them to be highly persuasive.

Being a great manipulator entails the ability to read the person you are trying to manipulate and then to exploit his or her weaknesses. Because the audience may not have the same weakness as the target, they do not buy into the act. But that is not important to the narcissist—the goal is only to manipulate one person. I was told a story by one of my research participants that illustrates this idea.

Jane was an only child growing up in the South. Her father was very ill when she was young. Jane loved her father and her fondest memories growing up were taking care of him. Unfortunately, Jane's father died when she was thirteen years old. Jane's mother did not deal well with his passing and started dating a variety of other men. She barely spoke about her late husband.

Jane grew up and was a real success. She graduated near the top of her high school class and then attended a prominent university. Her only real downfall, it seemed, was her choice of boyfriends. Of those, her biggest mistake was a guy named Peter.

Peter was a semi-big man on campus. He was an officer in his fraternity and was socially very popular. He was in a committed relationship with Jane. Well, Jane thought that it was committed, and she was faithful, but Peter would stray again and again. Every time he cheated, the same pattern was repeated. Jane would hear something from someone, call Peter, and tell him that she never wanted to see him again. Peter would then trek over to her apartment and start his routine.

Peter would knock and she would not let him in. Then he would plead and make a joke and she would open the door. Once in the apartment, Peter would say how sorry he was and promise that it would never ever happen again. He would say that he was worried that he had made the "biggest mistake of his life." Finally, he would look her deep in the eyes and say that he needed her. She was the only person who could keep him out of trouble, and he would be lost without her. At this point he would put a pleading look on his face and shed a few tears.

Jane could never resist the final one-two punch of need and tears. She would grudgingly take him back. Peter would be extremely nice for the next week or so. But then a party would come, he would start drinking, and the process would repeat itself.

Jane never let go of Peter—even though all her friends and family tried to convince her to dump him. Peter eventually found another woman. This broke Jane's heart.

Guys like this make everyone sick. They put on an act that is utterly transparent to everyone except the victim. In this last example, everyone knew Peter was a bad guy, except the woman that he had figured out how to manipulate. Like Jane, the narcissist's victims may buy the act again and again.

The other thing to notice is that Peter was able to find and exploit a big weakness in someone who was otherwise a really stable and successful woman. Jane needed to be needed. Peter sensed this vulnerability and exploited it as long as he wanted. This was acting for an audience of one and it worked.

One way to think about a narcissist is that he can be charming when he needs to be. He can act in the way that the situation demands—when everyone is having a good time, he will have a good time, and when everyone is sad, he can be sympathetic. He can play "hardball" and his ego can be bruised. But, no matter how a narcissists appears, the bottom line is that *he wants something*. Repeat: *He wants something*. It may be attention or admiration or power, but he does want something.

Self-deception is another key to narcissists' success. Narcissists are great manipulators. They can swiftly spot weaknesses in others. Narcissists have another advantage when it comes to deception and manipulation: they often believe their own story.

In the example with Peter and Jane, any outside observer would assume that Peter was a manipulative jerk. It is clear that Peter recognized Jane's weakness and used that to his own advantage. Peter was certainly aware of his manipulation, but my guess is that he really believed that he had at least some deep and real feelings for Jane. How is this possible? How could he have real feelings for Jane and constantly treat her so poorly? The answer is a bit complex and necessitates taking the perspective of the narcissist— in this example, Peter.

When you are a narcissist, it is not the case that you have the capacity to experience deep and caring feelings for other people, but choose instead to have shallow relationships. It also isn't that you have deep and warm connections with others, but forgo those for more selfish desires. Instead, narcissists do not feel the same connection with others that normal people feel. This lack of feeling is in part why they have shallow relationships. Here is the catch, however. Narcissists are not fully aware that they do not experience the same range of emotions that others do. So, narcissists interpret their shallow emotions as deeper ones. The case of narcissistic love that we discussed earlier is a case in point. Narcissists think that game playing *is* love. They feel excited and cocky and act in a cool, charming way and think, *Wow, this is a really good relationship full of true feelings!* [28]

Returning to the case of Peter and Jane, Peter was a player. His emotional instrument only played a few notes: excitement, power, and admiration. It did not play compassion, caring, or empathy. So, when he felt the rush of trying to win back Jane's adoration, Peter thought that those emotions were perhaps real love. He thinks, "Wow, this is a really good relationship!" He could say he loved her, and not really be lying. However, because there was no actual caring or compassion, it was easy for Peter to hurt Jane again and again, even though he supposedly had "deep" feelings for her.

In short, a narcissist lives in his own little world. His goal is to shape the world to make him look and feel special, important, excited, powerful. Romantic relationships are just another place to get these feelings. Deception is one of his best tricks for getting what he wants from his partners. Unfortunately, narcissists are professionals at the manipulation game. As hard as it is, you should trust his behavior more than his words, and trust the impressions of your friends and family more than your own.

Changing Places, Changing Faces

What is a narcissist to do? He loves being in relationships. He loves to look cool walking around with an attractive girlfriend. He likes her attention and the attention of others. He enjoys the feelings of power and control he has in the relationship. He gets excited by the dance of courtship. He likes to look good and thinks of himself as a "player," "stud," "ladies man," or, in the case of some marriages, a great "family man." He is not interested in commitment, compassion, connection, warmth, or any of the other things that people associate with love.

Alas, here is where a problem arises for the narcissist. The narcissist wants to keep the good times rolling for himself, but his girlfriend or wife wants a change. She might not want to listen to him talk about himself or flirt with other women. She might want him to care about her or support her emotional needs.

The narcissist has a choice to make. First, he can go the charm and manipulation route. He can cheat and be a jerk for a while and then turn on the charm in order to reestablish the relationship. This might work for some time, but grows tiring—especially after a better-looking woman is spied on the horizon. The second choice is to take off with another partner and start the whole process all over again.

This second choice is the one that often works best for the narcissist. He is charming and outgoing, so meeting new people is easy for him. His best bet is to leave the relationship that is growing troublesome and head off for greener pastures.

The result of this pattern of choices is a merry-go-round of new relationships. A narcissist "churns" his relationships in order to keep the fantasy going. He has to keep moving in order to keep the good times rolling. Think about the narcissists you know and this pattern will become apparent. Narcissistic guys keep their friends for a short time. Decent guys keep their friends for a long time. Here is a story that I was told by a friend that captures narcissists' readiness to change places and faces quite well.

Liz met Jake at a bar in Manhattan. Jake was an attractive guy and wore really nice clothes. Jake also carried himself well—he seemed so sure of himself. After a dizzy conversation Liz thought that there was some potential here. Jake told the story of how he had recently moved to New York after finishing law school at Duke. He was now working at a big-time city firm. Liz gave Jake her number before leaving the bar.

Three days later, Jake still had not called and Liz was about to give up on ever hearing from him. That Thursday, however, he did call and asked her to go out the following evening.

They met at a martini bar and spent the evening talking. He talked about how great his job was, but how busy it could get on some days. Jake made her laugh and she felt lucky to be out with him.

Liz was smitten and soon they were dating regularly. Jake was gone on many weekends because of his work, but when he was in town he went out with Liz. Liz was thinking that it might be time to introduce Jake to her parents.

There were some problems in the relationship, however. Jake never wanted Liz to meet his friends from work, although he did seem to know lots of people at the bars they frequented. Also, a couple of times women asked if she was serious about

Jake. When she said "yes" the women sort of rolled their eyes but did not say much else. Jake was flirtatious with other women, but she thought that he was just being nice.

One day she was out at lunch and saw a friend of Jake's. She said hello and they talked a bit about him. The friend mentioned that he did not see her at the bar last night. Liz said that there must be a mistake because Jake was working at the law firm last night. The friend got a perplexed look and said that Jake did not work at a law firm; he was a salesman at a clothing store.

Liz was troubled by this conversation to say the least. She confronted Jake that night about it. Jake came clean and said that he really started law school, but decided to go to New York instead. He also said that he had meant to tell her the truth, but that he was embarrassed and did not want to lose her. His eyes teared up and Liz felt sorry for him. She said everything was okay, but that he would have to spend more time with her if he was not working late. They did spend a lot of time together for a while, but soon Jake stopped calling. Liz went to the bar to look for him, but no one had seen him around in a while.

Liz was hurt, but she was able to talk with some of her friends and got over it relatively quickly. Six months later, Liz was out and saw Jake at a different bar with a different girl. Liz was disturbed by seeing him. She had not thought about him in a couple of months. Jake did not see Liz, and when he walked to the bathroom Liz went up to his girlfriend. She told the girl that Jake was not a lawyer and really was a jerk. Jake's new girl said, "I know he is not a lawyer. He is an investment banker, and we may get married." Liz told her again that Jake was not a good guy, but she just said that Liz was jealous. Liz left the bar and resolved not to think about Jake again.

Six months later, Liz did see Jake again. He was at a new bar in midtown with a different girl. They were sitting quietly against the wall just like Jake and Liz had when they first went out. Part of Liz wanted to say something, but she just left. She had her own life and did not want Jake in it.

Jake is a classic narcissist. He keeps acting in the same drama over and over. Jake feels good all the time. He always has a great looking girlfriend who thinks that he is a big deal. He goes out partying in the big city night after night. He is living the high life. People know who he is.

The problem with Jake's story is that it only works as long as the other actors believe in their roles. When they start catching on that they are just playing a part in Jake's drama, Jake has to find new actors for another production. In fact, I would speculate that during all those late nights when Jake was "working," he was actually setting up new scenes and new actors. This would serve to smooth the transition to his new drama when the current one falls apart. The casualties in Jake's drama are his various girlfriends. Jake hurts many women, but he can always find more.

We now have a better idea of narcissists and their approach to relationships. It boils down to the following:

1. It is all about the narcissists' needs and desires (status, power, sex, admiration).
2. Intimacy and caring are not high in the list of needs.
3. Narcissists have many skills and qualities that make them attractive—they are extroverted, confident, charming, appear successful, and are manipulative.

The big question, of course, is: Why would women ever get involved with a narcissist?

Chapter Three

Why Get Involved with a Narcissist?

Making a Big Entrance

If you have been involved with a narcissist—and thought afterwards "What was I thinking?"—you are not alone. I have heard this story many times. In our research on university undergraduates, roughly 75 percent report having dated narcissists. Remember, these are women between 18–21 years old and who have often not had a great deal of dating experience. Thus, it would be safe to assume that the numbers would be significantly higher for a slightly older age group.

The regret over dating narcissists is also highly prevalent. One of my favorite examples of this was in a research study. After a woman wrote about her experiences dating a narcissist and answered some questions, she wrote in large block letters: "WHY DID I DATE

HIM?" She was speaking for many women. For all the reasons discussed in the last section, narcissists are generally romantic mistakes. Not only that, but women tend to dwell on their relationships with narcissists—maybe the reason you are reading this book! Women keep wondering about what went wrong.

Not only is dating a narcissist common, but many women also report dating one narcissist after another. She does not intend to do this—all the experiences end up poorly—but she does it anyway. Furthermore, while she is dating a string of narcissistic jerks, she is missing out on dating one decent guy. Not only is there an emotional cost to dating narcissists, but there is also what economists call an *opportunity cost*—individuals miss out on many good dating opportunities.

So, why do women date narcissistic men? There are several reasons, and I will try to tackle each one in detail. But first, there are three very important points to highlight:

1. *Women generally do not know that narcissists are narcissists when they start dating them*. Narcissists do not have big "N's" on their shirts, or, as my wife once put it, narcissists do not come with warning labels. There are a few exceptions to this rule:

- A woman may sometimes think a guy is a narcissist or player with other women, but not necessarily with her.
- A woman may suspect that a guy is a narcissist, but not think about that because she is only interested in a short-term relationship.

- A woman may know that a guy is "cocky" or "charming," but not think that this involves a full-blown narcissistic pattern of behavior.

Generally, however, narcissists who are successful do not come right out and say that they are narcissistic pigs at the start of a relationship. That truth takes some time to emerge.

2. *Narcissists have many traits that are very attractive.* He has positive qualities like extroversion and confidence, and negative qualities like a tendency towards infidelity. In relationships, the positive qualities are usually the ones that you see first. If narcissists were totally unattractive, he wouldn't do the damage that he does.

3. *Women who date narcissists are not crazy.* The majority of women have had experiences with narcissistic men. The reason she has these experiences is that narcissists are really good at starting relationships. This is the same reason that sleazy salesmen are so good at selling and politicians are so good at getting votes.

Keep those three points in mind and let me start by discussing narcissists' initial approach to a relationship, which is one reason why we will be immediately attracted to narcissists. I like to think of this as the *Big Entrance*. Narcissists will show up with some flash and bravado when you meet them. He is confident and not socially anxious. He may tell a story about how successful he is: "Well, I'm just taking a short break from my job at the stock exchange. I can't quit when there is so much money being made." They may drop other impressive tidbits of information in their conversations: "Are you having a martini? Yes, that reminds me of the season I spent yachting on St. Martin." This sounds shallow (and my examples are a bit extreme), but, frankly, people are impressed by this type of self-promoting talk. Who is more attractive initially, a guy who says that he is a successful surgeon and spends two months a year in Tuscany, or a guy who says that he works in the medical field and gets a little traveling in when he has time? I am thinking Tuscany. In short, narcissists are not afraid to make a big entrance, and that can be attractive.

Does that mean that men who make big entrances should be avoided? Unfortunately, it is not that simple. Many people are self-confident and self-promoting when you first meet them. The reason is simple: We have positive first impressions of people who are self-promoting. It works, so many men do it. The difference is that narcissists do not stop the self-promotion, whereas normal men do.

Psychologist Dianne Tice has done research on the importance of self-promotion in first impressions. In her work she has consistently found that self-promotion works in the *short run*. She once used a simple example that really rang true for me. When she was in graduate school, she had a professor who announced during the first day of class that he had gone to Harvard Divinity School. All the students in the class were favorably impressed by this fact and thought that he was a pretty cool guy. Unfortunately, the professor kept mentioning Harvard Divinity School throughout the semester. "Yes, I studied that when I was at Harvard Divinity School." "Clearly, as a Harvard Divinity

School graduate..." The more he bragged about his academic background, the more unattractive he became. If he had mentioned it once or twice, he would have been perceived as a cool professor. He kept self-promoting, however, and managed to turn off the entire class. Narcissists are not good at stopping the act. Their self-promotion is an attractive trait at first, but later proves unattractive.[1]

Narcissists' attractiveness is even more basic than self-promotion. A lot of it has to do with the immediate, gut-level response people have to them. In a recent study, psychologists showed people thirty-second videos of strangers behaving in various ways. These people were then asked to rate how much they liked these strangers. What was amazing was that people liked the narcissists more than others—even after thirty seconds! This is largely a reflection of narcissists' extroversion and energy. We like people who are energetic—we don't as readily like people who are sullen or quiet.[2]

The attractive qualities of male self-promotion can also be seen in the animal kingdom. The classic example, of course, involves peacocks (although all sorts of animals will use different sorts of self-promotion strategies). Male peacocks have a large and brilliant cluster of tail feathers, which are displayed during mating season. He will extend his plumage and strut back and forth. Peahens find this quite appealing and will mate with males who display the best-looking feathers.

It is important to note that the peacock's displays are reserved for peahens. The peacock does not sit alone in front of a mirror and check out his bright tail feathers, nor does he show his friends how impressive his feathers can be. Peacocks do want to look good for peahens, but that is all.

Many men are like peacocks. These men want to look good in front of the opposite sex. Narcissists, however, are like peacocks for whom it is always mating season and everyone is a potential mate. He does not know when to put the feathers away.

I witnessed a wonderful example of this narcissistic approach to dating relationships. My uncle and I were having dinner in a pizza place in New Zealand's South Island. This is an area that is well known for its outdoor pursuits like hiking, white-water rafting, and fly fishing, and many of the patrons were visitors engaging in these activities.

At a table next to us were a man and woman who looked like they were on a date. Our guess was that they had both met on their respective vacations. The guy commenced talking as soon as they sat down. He talked about his adventurous travels, his outdoor life in Canada, and his future plans. I think that the woman got in two words. Still, she seemed highly impressed.

He kept talking. At one point in the meal, he started telling stories about ice climbing in Jasper, Canada. He even pulled out a map to show her where Jasper was. He then used one of my all-time favorite narcissistic lines: "Ice climbing is not for everyone; it takes a certain verve." My uncle and I almost laughed out loud. Still, he just kept going. It was clear two minutes into the discussion that the woman was interested in him, but he kept talking.

We spent much of our meal entertaining ourselves by imitating our ice-climbing friend, but he was too focused to hear us. When we finally left the restaurant, he was still talking. I thought that the woman still appeared interested, but I was not sure how long that would last.

At the end of the meal, his flagrant self-promotion did not make sense. He could have just told a few impressive stories, maybe actually listened to his date for a few minutes, and he would have been set. In retrospect, however, it is clear: *most men want to look good for women; narcissists also want to look good for themselves.* Our ice-climbing friend's show was not just to impress his companion. His show was to impress himself. He got to feel like a big deal, world traveler, and ice climber. *She was an excuse to tell the story to himself.* Does this make you want to laugh or cry?

In sum, a narcissist makes a big entrance in his romantic relationships. He is not afraid to talk about himself and his accomplishments. Unfortunately, other confident men also use the big entrance strategy, so initially it is difficult to differentiate the narcissists from the normals. The difference may be subtle. Narcissists want to be attractive to others, but the main goal is to make themselves feel powerful and important. He might tell you a story about his success and then repeat the story to anyone and everyone who will listen. Other men may strut their stuff in front of you, but not everyone else at the party. Likewise, narcissists—like my ice-climbing friend—may keep talking about himself long after he has piqued your interest. Other men will stop once he knows that you are attracted—his goal is simply to get you interested, not to inflate his own self-image. The big entrance can be very attractive, but it only works for a short time. Narcissists keep selling themselves, which eventually turns most people off. However, it may take a week, a month, or twenty years. I will talk about this satisfaction drop in detail later.

The Old Bait and Switch

Academic psychologists often think of relationships using the metaphor of economics. In many ways relationships involve a kind of exchange between two people. There are several things that can be exchanged in a relationship. These include social support, financial support, companionship, or learning about one's self or relationships.[3] For example, people will say things like, "It was a good relationship. He really taught me a lot about myself and about getting along in a relationship. I also think that I taught him a lot about himself. I also gave him support when he had some family problems."

This does not mean that people explicitly enter a relationship like a business negotiation. No one sits down and hammers out an agreement after looking at each other's balance sheets (prenuptial agreements being the emotionally tricky exception). Relationship formation is definitely more chemical and automatic than the standard business deal; however, people still have some sense of an exchange process in relationships. The exchange itself may be implicit or unconscious, but when it is violated, it can have negative consequences for the relationship. I will elaborate on this latter point in a moment.

Two of the classic elements "exchanged" in relationships are status and attractiveness. Traditionally, men offer status and security. Women offer youth and attractiveness. I do not want to sound overly traditional or sexist here. This model of the "dating marketplace" has changed a great deal with the increase of women's wealth and economic opportunity. Today you sometimes see wealthy women with handsome "boy toy" husbands, although this is still rare.

Whenever I talk about this in my class, I give the following example. Imagine that you see a very attractive woman out with a very unattractive man. What do you think? Usually someone will call out, "He is rich!" The class will laugh, but generally agree. Someone else will suggest that maybe he is a really nice guy and the other students will say something like, "yeah, sure."

I then present this scenario: Imagine that you see a very attractive man out with a very unattractive woman? The class is always stumped by this. Someone will usually call out, "It's his sister!" or "He's gay!" This may lead to a laugh but does not address the question. Someone will then suggest that maybe she is really nice, to which the rest the students will respond with "sure she is...." The truth is that the class has great difficulty imagining an unattractive woman with a very attractive man.

This little exercise suggests that the exchange of men's wealth and status for women's youth and beauty is alive and well in today's culture. People can understand an unattractive rich man with an attractive woman, because this seems like a reasonable exchange. They have trouble imagining a man trading his looks for a woman's wealth and status.

I also want to offer an additional point. We are talking about status, wealth, and physical attractiveness. While these are important attributes in attracting a romantic partner, they are not the most important. In study after study, the most important traits rated by men and women are kindness and a sense of humor. People really want to be around others who are nice to them and who can make them laugh. That said, let's return to the exchange of status and physical beauty.

Exchange relationships can be great. We might call these successful exchanges "Win-Win" exchanges. A man with some social status and a good personality marries a nice and attractive woman and both parties win. Unfortunately, not all exchanges work out as nicely. One of the big problems in exchange relationships is that people cheat. They misrepresent what they are giving you or what they expect in return. Certain types of salesmen are notorious for this.

One of the classic sales tricks is known as the *bait and switch*. The bait and switch essentially involves offering to exchange a certain desirable item (the bait) and then replacing the desirable item with a less desirable item at the last minute (the switch). This strategy has three benefits to the seller who uses it. First, the bait will lure customers to try to deal with you. Second, once customers agree to an exchange with the bait, they become committed to the exchange. Thus, they are not likely to back out when the switch takes place. Finally, if the switch is effective, the seller ends up with much more out of the exchange than the customer.

Let me give an example that might help to clarify this. A car dealership will advertise a fantastic price on a new car, say a new Mustang with all the extras. This is the bait. The potential buyer will be lured to the dealership because of this bait. After the negotiation process for the car begins, the switch will take place. This typically happens in a couple ways. For example, after the buyer is committed to the car, the salesman will say that the price does not include various shipping, accessory, and storage fees that add up to a significant amount of money. Alternately, the seller will say that the desirable Mustang that was advertised is no longer available, but that there is another one that is almost as good available. Buyers often still buy the car even after the switch, because they are now committed to the car. They have fantasized for days about driving a new Mustang, they have told their friends how great the Mustang is, etc. The bottom line is that the salesman makes a profitable sale by promising a lot out front, but not delivering all that he initially promised.

This same bait and switch tactic is used in dating relationships. Individuals will promise a lot, but after some commitment is reached, he will only deliver a small part of what he initially promised. Both women and men take part in the bait and switch.

One easy place to see the bait and switch is in the realm of physical appearance. How is this possible? Individuals promise one physical appearance and then deliver another. This is not as difficult to do as it may seem. Women spend billions of dollars each year on products that enhance their appearance or hide deficits. These include cosmetics, control-top pantyhose, and even plastic surgery. At the movies this weekend, we stood in line next to a young woman on what looked like a first date. Her silhouette would have made Barbie blush. My wife leaned over and whispered, "Nice socks!" My wife saw through the bait and switch. The woman's date (and maybe a few other guys at the theater) was still staring at the bait.

Men, of course, augment their physical appearance as well. For example, men may "pump up" with weights before going out so that they look stronger than they actually are (as a rule, men overestimate the attractiveness of muscles to women). Men also are starting to use plastic surgery. They purchase more masculine chins, bigger pectoral muscles, or larger calves via the magic of silicone. No, I am not making this up.

So how does all this tie back into narcissism? Narcissists also use a bait and switch strategy. He promises one thing in a relationship, and once a degree of commitment is achieved, he really gives another. Narcissists promise sophistication, looks, and social status. He carries himself as a popular, successful, important, and good-looking individual. Like all good salesmen, he can turn on the charm and that helps to sell the illusion. As we know, however, narcissists are not more successful or important or even better looking than anyone—they are just experts at selling themselves that way.

Narcissists are salesmen who sell an inflated image of themselves. He lures women in with the promise of dating a special, popular, important guy. The switch is subtle. It is the gradual replacement of the illusion with the reality. A woman finds out that her narcissistic boyfriend is not as successful at his job as he claims.

He does not have the famous friends that she thought he did. His Mercedes is leased and he is two months behind on the payment. (In fact, I heard one story about an ex-boyfriend in law school who was upset because he didn't have the highest lease payment in his class!)

Once again we see that women do not date narcissists for who they are. Instead, women date narcissists for the person whom the narcissist pretends to be. This is not because women are stupid. Rather, narcissists use a standard salesman's trick—the bait and switch—to sell themselves to potential romantic partners. Narcissists advertise themselves as BMWs with all the accessories at a low, low price. In reality, the engine is not quite as powerful as it sounds, the leather seats are really pleather, and the car is being sold to ten other buyers at the same time. As we will discuss later, the best way to avoid this is to find out a person's reputation. Chances are, if he is lying to you, he has lied to someone else.

The Illusion That Other People Are Like You

As we have seen, narcissists make a big entrances in relationships. The narcissist also uses a bait and switch strategy where he presents an image of a successful guy who is charming and focused on a woman. This guy is later switched for a self-centered jerk once a woman is sufficiently committed. Narcissists can be very good at manipulating people. He has practiced this strategy for most of his life, and, like any successful con man, does manage to convince others of all sorts of untruths.

There is another advantage that narcissists have for manipulating potential romantic partners. Women (indeed, most people) have the illusion that other people are like them. Social psychologists have a fancy term for this, the *false consensus effect*.[4]

The false consensus effect is found in all sorts of places. Smokers overestimate the number of people who smoke. Democrats and Republicans both overestimate the number of people in the country who share their views. They use terms like "Moral Majority" to describe a group that is not really a majority. People who have a certain tastes in clothes overestimate the number of people who share their tastes.

This false consensus is largely a result of the fact that we surround ourselves with people who are similar to us. When you smoke, for example, you spend a good deal of time standing outside your office building or in bars surrounded by other smokers. You obviously assume that many people smoke. When you quit smoking and stop hanging out with smokers, you soon assume that only a few people smoke. Your beliefs about people are influenced by your experience.

The false consensus effect also affects romantic relationships. We think that other people are like us. Most women (and men as well) are nice. They have the desire to take others' perspectives and resist hurting others. This is especially true with people whom they date. Most women care about their romantic partners.

The assumption that most women make, then, is that the people they date will have the same perspective of relationships. Women assume that when they date someone, that person will care about them, take their perspective, and resist hurting them. Most of the time this assumption holds true—most men are pretty decent. When narcissists enter the picture, however, women's default assumptions lead them into trouble.

The following is a story I heard from an acquaintance, and it is similar to several stories I have heard in my research.

Shawn had several previous boyfriends. These relationships had ended for benign reasons—Shawn had attended two universities and her job required her to live in several large cities. Nevertheless, Shawn considered her relationships with men to be positive, and she still had friendly, nonromantic relationships with two ex-boyfriends. It was safe to say that Shawn was a nice woman who had dated several reasonably nice guys.

She met Rex when she was out with friends after a late night at the office. Rex was an accountant at a major firm and was auditing a company in the area. He seemed like a nice, attractive, and successful guy when they first met. He was fun to talk to and she felt a twinge of attraction.

Shawn called Rex up the next day and asked him out—she was not the kind to wait around. They went out the next weekend and had a great time. In retrospect, the only troubling sign was that Rex seemed to be flirting with the waitress. At the time, however, Shawn did not expect that type of behavior and did not notice it.

After a few more nights out they were officially dating. Shawn thought things were great. She did not know if Rex was "the one," but he seemed like a good guy and she enjoyed seeing him.

One week Rex just stopped calling. She left messages a couple of times and he did not return her calls. She even went by the company where he was working, but they told her that he was with a new client.

She tried to contact him for two weeks. She left several messages on his home and cell phone. She even emailed. She was beginning to worry that something might have happened to him.

A month after he "vanished," she saw Rex having lunch at a restaurant. She felt this immediate sense of relief—she did not even feel anger—and went over to talk to him. When Rex saw her, he just looked annoyed. Shawn was confused by this. She said that she was worried about him and wondered what had happened to him. Rex just gave her a dismissing look and said that he was "over it."

Shawn was a bit shocked and confused by this. She just backed away from the table and left the restaurant. That week she talked to her friends and she started getting angry. She was also confused. Why on earth hadn't he talked to her if there was a problem? Why didn't she see that he was such an ass? Why was it so hard to get over this relationship?

Shawn is a nice woman who got involved with a narcissist. She was taken in by him because she thought that most guys were nice, like her. Indeed, this had always been Shawn's experience in her past dating relationships. She was totally unaware of what a self-centered jerk (to put it mildly) Rex was until the very end.

She just did not imagine that a guy would treat her with such callous disregard. She had never seen it happen and it did not make sense. If Rex did not want to date anymore, he could have just talked to her. It happens all the time and she would have handled it fine.

Shawn's confusion was totally understandable. Many women are confused after dating narcissistic men and are cursed with thinking about the relationship for a long time. Whenever we run across something that makes no sense, we ruminate about it. We want to make sense out of our world. (I elaborate on this later in the book.) The questions Shawn asked were also pretty typical of women in this situation. I will try to answer them.

Why did Rex not talk to her if there was a problem with the relationship? The answer is that Rex is totally self-centered. He no longer wanted to be in the relationship. He probably met someone else, but there is no way of knowing. He had no interest in making the relationship work. The easiest way for Rex to deal with Shawn was to blow her off. Shawn's feelings were not part of Rex's mental calculations.

Why didn't she see that he was such an ass? Shawn expected guys to be relatively decent. This was how Shawn approached the relationship and how most of the men that she had dated in the past acted. Rex seemed nice at first. He was charming and seemed interested, so Shawn assumed that he was a decent guy.

Narcissists prey off women's expectations that men will treat them with some respect. Narcissists act like good guys for a while, and then reveal their self-centered nature. If all men were narcissists, this strategy would not work—women would expect it. Because only a minority of men are narcissists, the narcissists are effectively able to exploit women.

One way to think about this is to use a metaphor from high school biology class. When there are creatures in nature that are successful, a *mimic* will often develop to take advantage of the situation. For example, there is a little fish that lives in the mouth of certain large grouper (sea bass). The grouper do not eat this little fish because it cleans excess food from the grouper's teeth. The two species live in harmony and trust. Unfortunately, another fish has evolved to mimic the helpful fish. The mimic looks a lot like the helpful fish and the grouper will let it swim into its mouth without eating it. When the mimic manages to get into the grouper's mouth, however, it does not help the grouper. Instead, it takes a large bite out of the grouper's mouth and swims away.

A narcissist is also a mimic. He mimics the courtship behaviors of nice men. When he earns a woman's trust, however, he does some damage and then takes off.

⌄ *Why was it so hard to get over this relationship?* Relationships with narcissists are especially hard to get over for many women. There are several reasons for this. First and foremost, a narcissist is callous. He does not care about people deeply, even though he may act like he does. When a narcissist does something hurtful, it often does not make sense. Why would this guy treat me so poorly? Is it me? Did he meet someone else? The answer is that he is a narcissist and he does not care about anyone but himself, but because women are often not aware of this, they keep turning the relationship over and over in their heads trying to find an answer.

At a deeper and more emotional level, narcissists also violate women's trust in both men and in their own judgment. Women who are taken advantage of sometimes start to doubt their own understanding of the world. At the extremes, this can even lead to depression. Finally, women (and men) who are hurt often will seek an apology from the person who hurt them. Along with the apology, it is also beneficial to see some display of remorse. Think about it. When someone hurts you, you want them to say that they are sorry, to mean it, and to feel badly about what they did. If this happens, it allows you to forgive and to heal. Narcissists, however, generally cannot do this because (a) he is not sorry, and (b) he does not feel remorse. This can make it tough to move on from the relationship.

In order to get over relationships with narcissists you need to remember that narcissists are not like you or most men. Although they may act like they care, they do not. This is who they are and—to put it bluntly—it really sucks. There is no deeper explanation to be found.

I should also note that there is a similar and almost opposite problem that occurs with people who have been burned time and time again. Just like the smoker who has been surrounded by smokers, this person has been surrounded by dishonest men for much of her life. Not surprisingly, her expectation is that "all men are pigs." She expects men to be dishonest and thus does not distinguish well between decent guys and narcissists. I don't know if narcissists can spot these women or not, but they do take advantage of them. This, of course, reinforces the view that all men are bad, and the pattern repeats itself. Women with this view can get stuck in a cycle of relationships with narcissists from which escape is difficult.

By way of conclusion, I would like to reaffirm the notion that not all men are pigs. Men definitely have a slightly greater desire to philander than do women, but many men enjoy and function quite well in relationships. In fact, men on average fall in love more quickly than women and get greater psychological and physical health benefits from committed relationships (i.e., marriage). Married men live longer and are happier. Men also identify fewer problems in their ongoing romantic relationships than do women. Men's tendency is, on average, to be content with things the way they are. Yes, some men are definitely pigs, but certainly not all. The key is to spot and avoid pig-like men when possible, and when you do get "swined," realize that it is just a narcissist being a narcissist. We will discuss more on this in the next chapter.

Narcissists Try Harder (or, the Myth That All the Good Men Are Taken)

Who do we date? It may seem that the process is somewhat random. We think that people just show up in our life willy-nilly. For good or for bad, however, this is not how it works most of the time. In particular, there are two big factors that predict who you will end up dating.

The first rule is that you end up dating people with whom you spend time. This includes co-workers, classmates, friends of friends, and others in your social circle. On TV shows, women continually date men whom they meet on the street. This does not happen that often in real life. If people do date strangers, they are most often people who are part of their usual routine, for example, someone who goes to the same nightspot or shops at the same market.[5]

The second rule is that women in our society end up dating the men who ask them out. Even in modern times, women rarely ask out men. Women will hint, flirt, and look interested. In fact, many anthropologists and psychologists argue that it is actually women, not men, who initiate the courtship process. Even so, a woman will rarely formally ask a man out—that is up to the man.[6]

Combining these two rules, we reach the following conclusion: The men you will date are men who you see socially or at work and who are willing to ask you out.

What does this have to do with narcissism? Based on these two rules, it is clear that, all things being equal, narcissists are going to be much more likely to ask women out than "nice guys." Think of the typical narcissist—he is extroverted, outgoing, cocky, and flirtatious. He is not going to sit at home alone, he will be out and about socially, and he will not be afraid to hit on any woman who strikes his fancy.

I had an acquaintance in college who perfectly fit this profile. He was out every night at a bar or a party and he had no fear in approaching women. He used to say, "If you ask out twenty women and nineteen say no, there is still one that says yes." Sure, he got turned down time after time, but there were still plenty of women who went out with him. He could be charming and would lie quite a bit. Eventually, he got a reputation as a "ladies man" and most women learned to avoid him—many were even disgusted by him—but there were always new women in town and his strategy kept working. He never kept a girlfriend for long. Obviously he was not searching for a deep and committed relationship, so he never found one.

I had other friends, however, who were the exact opposite. They would stay at home many nights because they were not constantly drawn to social action and excitement. They were not recluses or shy. They did enjoy parties, but they often enjoyed spending time with a few good friends rather than with many strangers. They would be attracted to one woman rather than many, and often be nervous about asking her out. Even if the woman really liked them, they would be so afraid of blowing it that it would be a long time before they really approached her. This makes sense. When you are a narcissist and do not value women, rejection is not that terrible. When you are a nice guy and really like someone, rejection hurts. When these guys did enter relationships, they were usually long and committed. They were not cheating all the time. The truth is, however, that they often were not in relationships.

Now imagine that you were at the university at this time. Who would you date? You would probably want to date the "nice guys" if you were interested in a long-term relationship. However, you may not have the chance to meet these guys, and even if you did, you might not think that they were interested in you. In contrast, you would definitely come into contact with my narcissistic friend—perhaps even during your first month at school. He would definitely be interested, he would appear charming, and he would probably ask you out. You would be new in town and interested in dating someone, so you might say yes. You would go out a couple times and then he would reveal what a jerk he was. You would regret the relationship and wish that you could find a nice guy somewhere; but, when you went out at night you would keep running into narcissistic men. The nice guys would not be flirting with everyone at the party. They might even be at home.

I heard someone say once that picking up women is a "twenty-four-hour-a-day job." This seems to capture the narcissists' approach. A narcissist tries harder. He approaches dating like a job—a sales job. He may make cold call after cold call and wait for a few of the calls to pay off. Like any good salesman, narcissists are accustomed to and can handle minor rejection. When the narcissist gets rejected, he can think of all the women who would say yes and that keeps him going. The more sales he gets, the better he has done. A lot of guys are like this when they are young, but they grow out of it. Narcissists stay this way.[7]

The nice guys out there are not like salesmen. It is not a numbers game for them. They are not trying to tally up women. They become attracted to one woman and will pursue only her. They are usually not as blunt about the pursuit as narcissists. They will take their time in the hope that things will work out. For them it is not about ego, but about relating to another person.

Where will narcissists and nice guys flourish? Narcissists' "numbers game" approach will work best in an environment where people do not know each other and there is a lot of turnover. That is, men and women move in and move out rapidly. The first year at college is a great example of this. Women move in from all over the place, they do not have many friends, and they are a bit naïve. This is a perfect environment for narcissists to thrive. They will try to pick up any woman who looks lost or alone. The narcissist will be successful time and time again. The women will eventually wise-up to the narcissist's tactics; however, fortunately for the narcissist, another group of women will come in the next year.

Another place where this seems to be effective is big cities with lots of new faces and relationship turnover. This is one of the reasons why shows like *Sex and the City* take place in New York. People often will move to the big city in search of a job or an interesting life, but they may know only a few people. As they say, even with all the people, New York is the loneliest place in the world. Narcissists will thrive in these environments; they will pick out every new female face at a bar and give it a shot. It may not work often, but it will work enough.

Nice guys may get lost the first year of college or in big cities. They will thrive in smaller towns or in the later years of college when people get to know each other. When people are not always coming and going, the nice guys will thrive. Why? Because with a decent guy, the more people who know him and know about him, the more positively he will be perceived. This takes time, because these guys are not spending all their energy promoting themselves. It takes time for the news to get out.

Now imagine a narcissist in a small town. His act may work in high school, but pretty soon everyone will see through him. He might think he is a big deal, but other people will know the truth. Word gets out in a small town. There will not be new women year after year to try out his act on. The small town narcissist will have to tone down his approach, find women who are really desperate, or pack up and move to L.A.! Narcissists in small towns are likely to get mean or depressed because their games will not be played as easily.

There is a final message to glean from this discussion. Women—especially in new social environments—are likely to vastly overestimate the number of narcissistic men who are out there. Every time they are out they will be approached by narcissists. They will believe that most single men are narcissistic jerks because this is what they will see. The nice guys who are single do not make themselves known. These same women will also see that their friends who are married or who are in committed relationships are mostly with decent guys. This is because the narcissistic jerks out there are less likely to commit—they are spending their time hitting on every woman they see!

After this has gone on for a while, women reach the unavoidable conclusion that *all the good men are taken*. It makes perfect sense that women would believe this. Their married friends are with good men, and the narcissistic men are the ones they meet socially night after night. Fortunately, this is not true. It is simply a result of the fact that narcissists try harder.

Unfortunately, if women falsely believe that all the good men are taken, there can be several bad consequences. First and foremost, women may become discouraged with all men. They may simply give up on men or on relationships. Even worse, they may start putting up with narcissists' nonsense in relationships. Women in this situation may figure that narcissistic behavior is the best that they can expect. Finally, women may start to believe that relationships are "supposed to be this way" in the "sophisticated" big city. Shallow transitory relationships may seem sophisticated or exciting on *Sex and the City*, but they are ultimately not sufficient or sustaining. Even the sophisticated and shallow Samantha ends up getting hurt by a narcissist, Richard. We will discuss this issue further in the next section.

Addicted to Drama and Excitement

One explanation for attraction to narcissists involves the desire for drama and excitement. Some women see the ideal relationship as being exciting, dramatic, sophisticated, and arousing. If you just find a nice and decent guy and have a reasonably good relationship, you feel that something is missing. There is no staying up late worried about things falling apart or fantasizing about how things might turn out. There are no endless conversations with friends trying to interpret his words and behavior. There is no feeling of sophistication or coolness. At some level, the experience of the drama and excitement is more important than the actual romantic partner. I remember someone describing a friend by saying that "she loves being in love." This statement captures in part the drama and excitement that narcissists sometimes supply.

My hunch is that this desire for high drama and excitement in relationships is linked to things that we see in today's media. Something goofy has happened in our culture. Everything has gotten faster and, at the surface at least, more exciting or arousing. Music videos are a great example of this. A video never just shows somebody singing a song with one or two camera angles. Today, the person sings and dances and we get to watch from fifteen different camera angles that change every one and a half seconds. First a normal shot, then a shot from above, then a shot in grainy black and white, then a shot with a different outfit and backdrop. Then the fireworks go off for a little excitement. This entire process will take six seconds.

I am not trying to discount the talent and effort that goes into one of these videos. This is hard work. The point is that if we compare, say, Britney Spears today to the music videos of yesteryear, you will see a huge difference. Think about one of the old dance clips of Fred Astaire and Ginger Rogers. They used few camera angles and there were no flames or fireworks. The biggest excitement came when someone danced with a mop.

Basically, over the last fifty years, the popular media has dramatically increased the amount of action and movement. We, as viewers, get bored with two camera angles, so we get five, we get bored with that and then we get fifteen. It is very much like an addiction. We can get hooked on the action and we need bigger and bigger doses.

The push to increased arousal and drama has also occurred in television. Many of the most popular television shows center on romantic relationships. These are rarely simple or positive relationships. Usually there is crisis after crisis. We need this in order to be entertained. These are the times when people are bathed in a rose-colored light and everything is possible. Unfortunately, this never lasts—we are not made that way.

My intention is not to attack the entertainment industry. There are shows about healthy relationships, and troubled relationships have been an important part of creating drama for centuries. Shakespeare's great plays had plenty of disturbed or drama-infused relationships (Ophelia and Hamlet, Romeo and Juliet, Beatrice and Benedick).

The point is that, on occasion, people in the real world approach relationships in search of excitement and drama. They think that the stuff that they see on MTV is real. They think they want emotional intimacy when what they really want is the drama and excitement of the early stages of romantic infatuation. I sometimes think about this as "drama-lust." People see their romantic life as a great drama just like on TV.

This approach to relationships leads to an attraction to surface elements over substance dramatically and this is where narcissists flourish. The following story captures somewhat the addiction to drama.

Julie was an account manager at a consulting firm in a major West Coast city. Julie was successful at her job and had several friends. Some were from college, and some were people whom she had met through her work. Most people would describe Julie as "totally together" or "doing great." Julie thought of herself in this way as well. She thought that she had outgrown the suburbs where she grew up and now was living the good life.

Part of Julie's sense of sophistication was based on the men she had dated. These men included a successful attorney, an assistant to the mayor, and a somewhat well-known actor with whom she had gone to several parties where movie stars were in attendance. These relationships always had their ups and downs. The way that Julie felt when she was at a party on a boat with one of these men or when one of these men pulled up at her apartment in a new Jaguar, more than made up for the forgotten phone calls or lack of desire to commit.

Julie secretly felt bad for (and somewhat better than) her friends who had already gotten married and even started families. She liked their husbands well enough; they were nice men who had good jobs. However, she did not think that these types of men were up to her standards. They were not pushing the envelope and striving for great things. They did not go to popular restaurants and have sophisticated friends. Instead, they were content to raise kids and spend their weekends doing yard work. This was fine for her friends, but not enough for her.

The funny thing was, Julie's close friends saw the situation from an opposite perspective. They thought that Julie was acting like she was in high school and was dating the quarterback of the football team. Sure, the parties sounded fun, but they were not "real." It was like pretending you were on a TV show rather than having a real relationship. They guessed that Julie was not truly satisfied with her relationships. They tried to talk to her about the issue, but they never were able to get through to her.

After a few years of living like this, Julie started to have doubts of her own. Her friends were starting to have families, even the movie stars were having families, and Julie felt the urge to settle down herself. Soon, the idea of getting married became more and more important to her. Julie, however, thought about marriage in the same dramatic terms as she thought about the rest of her relationships. She pictured herself in an elaborate wedding ceremony where everyone and everything looked perfect. She would have great photos taken. Her honeymoon would be in Bora Bora or Tuscany. She thought that she would like a great house and maybe she would drive a Range Rover. She would take up tennis, and she and her husband would spend romantic weekends in Santa Barbara or Palm Springs.

The problem for Julie was that it was difficult to find a husband who fit the bill. She eventually fell for Howard. He was a talker—he talked about his company, how much money his deals were making, and how he preferred the Four Seasons to other hotels. They spent many evenings out at restaurants and shows. Julie knew he was the guy.

Julie's new dream eventually came true and they got married. In the first year, she realized that the romance would not last forever. Howard was working all the time, and she felt that she was used as a prop at parties. She got pregnant and had twins. Julie decided to focus all her energy on their success. She would dress them up and hang pictures of them all over the house. She suspected that Howard was having affairs, but kept her attention on the kids. She still had a great house and what appeared to be the perfect family.

Julie's friends heard from Julie less and less. They would get a big Christmas card with a photo of the kids, but that was about it. When they did talk, the topic was always how the family was going to Hawaii for Easter and how well the kids were doing in school. Julie seemed to have the perfect life—it was like a movie—but it did not seem fulfilling.

Julie never felt that things were real unless everything was special and exciting. She designed her life like a movie set. There were lots of props, but not a lot of substance. She dated a string of narcissistic men and finally married a narcissist. She was attracted to these men because they supplied drama and excitement to her life. They took her out to great places and they knew all the right people. They also did not really know or care to know Julie; she was more of a player in their life drama. The men were always the stars of the show, however. They were interested and attentive for a while, but then moved on once the act was over. Even her husband was only interested in looking like a successful family man. The relationship was not the important part.

Many women are like Julie. They love the drama and excitement of romantic relationships. They thrive in the infatuation stage, but have trouble experiencing real intimacy in relationships. Almost everyone agrees that infatuation is great. It feels wonderful. It is exciting. Most people, however, know that real intimacy feels good as well, and it lasts and can grow stronger over time. Infatuation is short-term and gets weaker over time, but not everyone has learned this lesson.

Women like Julie are drawn to narcissistic men. They are flashy, they can be charming and dramatic, and they do best in the early stages of relationships. The problem is that the drama of relationships with narcissists ends sooner than a season of sitcoms. In fact, this is the standard pattern of relationships with narcissists.

The Great Satisfaction Drop

It might be wise at this point to quickly summarize this chapter thus far. Women are often attracted to narcissistic men. There are several reasons for this. The biggest factor is that *women are attracted to narcissists because a narcissist does not announce that he is a narcissist when he begins a relationship.*

Narcissists may use a *bait and switch* strategy to gain women's affection. Narcissists may make a big entrance, present the aura of status, use charm, and offer a relationship filled with great drama and excitement. Narcissists are like wolves in Golden Retriever's clothing. They appear wonderful, but this is only a disguise.

The illusion does not last, however. True insight into the narcissist's personality occurs with time. They are seen as selfish, unfaithful, and uncaring. Once the real narcissist has stepped forward, the relationship takes a downward plunge. I think of this as the *great satisfaction drop*.

Rather than begin by presenting an example from a dating relationship, I would like to talk about results from a terrific study that looked at this satisfaction drop in groups of strangers. This study was conducted by Dr. Del Paulhus at the University of British Columbia. The participants in the study were not romantically involved, but the experience is very similar.[8]

A small group of students who were all strangers had their narcissism scores measured. The results were not revealed to them or any of the other students. The students were then asked to spend an hour interacting with each other. Like any group of students who have just met, they introduced themselves and talked about some of their interests. They told each other what their majors were, what they were doing that weekend, and perhaps what they thought of the psychology experiment that they were in. At the end of the session, the students rated each other on a range of personality traits. This included how exciting the others were, how extroverted and sociable they were, and, of course, how much they each liked each of the others.

The results of the first session were just as the researchers expected. The narcissists were well liked by all. The narcissists were seen as exciting, sociable, and energetic. In fact, students tended to like the narcissists *more* than the other students. What is neat is that this finding is consistent with what we have discussed regarding narcissists' dating relationships. Narcissists make great first impressions. They are exciting, charming, and very energetic.

Now, here is where the study gets really interesting. The same students were brought back for a one-hour meeting week after week. They were placed in a room and were allowed to interact for the entire hour. At the end of each session, the students rated each other on the same scales.

What would you guess happened to the ratings of the narcissists? Would the narcissists still be well liked after seven weeks? In contrast, would people learn to see through the narcissists' illusion and begin to dislike them? As you may have guessed, the latter occurred. Over time, the students learned to dislike the narcissists. By the end of the six sessions, the narcissists were liked *less* than the other students. They were still seen as energetic, but they were no longer seen as exciting or sociable. The narcissistic spell was broken in six weekly meetings. After getting to know the narcissists, they become less likable and attractive—the great satisfaction drop.

From a scientific perspective, it would be nice to do a study like Dr. Paulhus's with dating couples. Unfortunately, we cannot ethically ask people to date narcissists and then study them for seven weeks! So my colleagues and I tried a different approach. Our goal was to see if we could find evidence of the great satisfaction drop in dating couples.

We used a very simple approach. We asked people to write stories about two of their previous dating relationships. One of the stories was about a narcissistic dating partner. The other story was about a non-narcissistic dating partner. After writing the stories, people answered several questions about their relationship, including how immediately they were attracted to their partner, how satisfied they were at the beginning of the relationship, and how satisfied they were at the end of the relationship. The results we found were even stronger than we expected.[9]

I will start by describing the stories about the non-narcissistic or "normal" dating partners. In most cases, women reported that it took a little bit of time to become attracted to their partner. Perhaps they had known him for a while. When they began dating the partner, however, they were very satisfied. They usually thought that their partner was nice and caring, with a good sense of humor. When they broke up with their partner, they were only a little less satisfied. They still thought that their partner was a decent individual. The relationships ended because one of the individuals moved, or they "just grew apart."

The stories about the narcissistic dating partners were very different. First, women usually reported becoming attracted very quickly to the narcissistic men. They would see them for the first time at a social event and feel drawn to them. At the beginning of the relationship, women reported being very satisfied with the narcissistic partners. They thought the narcissists were terrific. By the end of the relationship, the satisfaction with the narcissistic partners had plummeted. Most of the women were totally fed up with their narcissistic boyfriends and they often did not know why they dated them. The reasons were varied, but all were negative. During the relationship, women realized that their narcissistic boyfriends were selfish and self-centered, arrogant, and cocky. They were manipulative. They also flirted with other women and were even unfaithful. In some cases, they were abusive and violent. In short, the attraction to the narcissist started out burning brightly but burned out as the relationship progressed.

I will present excerpts from two stories to clarify the difference between dating narcissists and non-narcissists. Of course, the names and other identifying information have been altered.

I met Jim during the first month I was at the University. We met at a fraternity party. I thought he was the cutest guy that I had ever seen. He came up to me and we started dancing. I remember that for the first time I felt like I was really in college.

Jim and I got together again the next weekend. I saw him in the quad and he told me to meet him at another party. After that, the relationship was great. We were together every weekend.

Things started to change around fall break. He went to Florida with some friends and didn't invite me. When they got back, he didn't call. I went over to see him the weekend after he got back and he was just mean. He told me to get out of his house in front of a bunch of his friends. I couldn't believe the change. I saw him the next weekend and tried to talk to him. He blew me off and later I saw him dancing with another girl. I guess I didn't see what an ass he was until right then.

I decided to stop calling him right then and that was that.

* * *

I met Steve at a game of intramural ultimate Frisbee. We talked a bit and he seemed to have a good sense of humor. I saw him at a party at a friend's apartment that weekend. We talked a little more. He seemed like a nice guy, but I didn't know anything would happen. Later that night he asked me if he could call me and I said, "Yes."

He did call the next weekend and we went out to a movie. We had a lot of fun and I found myself liking him more and more. Pretty soon we were dating. I really liked Steve. We did all sorts of fun things together and he was always a nice guy. At times I was worried that he might be "too nice," but he never was like that.

When summer came up, he decided that he would go to Europe and I was going to move back to my parent's and do an internship. Neither of us really wanted to break up, but we both wanted to do different things. At that point we decided we would be friends and see what happened. I met another guy at home and Steve did meet a girl in Europe.

When we got back, we stayed friends and we still are friends to this day.

I am sure that you can guess who the narcissist is. It is Jim. He came across as a popular and attractive guy. She was attracted immediately. Dating him was exciting, but the relationship was a disaster. The great satisfaction drop occurred after only a few weeks. Jim went from "great guy" to "ass" after one weekend in Florida. Relationship satisfaction dropped—right off a cliff. Fortunately this student did not waste a great deal of time pining away after Jim.

Steve, on the other hand, was not a narcissist. The relationship with Steve lacked that immediate attraction. Yes, she liked Steve when she first met him, but the chemical "zing" was not there. Instead, her attraction to Steve grew over time. Dating Steve was not totally exciting, but it ultimately was more satisfying than dating Jim. Even though the relationships with Steve ended, they still liked each other a lot and remained friends.

You may have read these two stories and thought, "Sure Steve seems like a good guy, but Jim was a lot more attractive. He was popular and always at parties. I would still want to date him." This may seem true at first—in fact, narcissists everywhere are banking on this interpretation—but if you think about it a minute, the opposite is true. Jim acted cool, but he was a jerk who hung out with a bunch of his fraternity buddies. This was probably a big source of self-esteem for him. His big adventure was going to Florida with these same friends. In contrast, Steve was an outgoing guy who did not seem to need others to hang around and boost his self-esteem. His adventure was going to Europe and he was willing to talk to his girlfriend and see if they could work it out before they parted ways. He was able to have a close relationship with a woman and still be friends afterwards. He did not need to publicly humiliate his girlfriend in order to end the relationship.

Sometimes the best way to see things happen in relationships is with pictures or graphs rather than words. We tried this approach in another study similar to the one just described.[10] For this study, we asked individuals to graph their relationships with narcissists and non-narcissists. This is not very complex (I will explain how to do it for your relationship in the next section). Basically, all people did was draw a line that represented how satisfied they were across their relationship from the first week to the last. The results were stunning. As you can see in Figure 1, the satisfaction with the narcissistic partners (the dashed line with triangles) is actually higher at the beginning of the relationship than that of the satisfaction with the non-narcissistic partners (the solid line with circles). In the first couple months of dating, people found narcissists to be more satisfying dating partners than non-narcissists! Then, a big shift happens: the relationships with the narcissists become less and less satisfying, but the non-narcissists become more satisfying. By around four months into the relationships, the relationships with the narcissists have become miserable, but the relationships with non-narcissists are just hitting their peak of satisfaction.

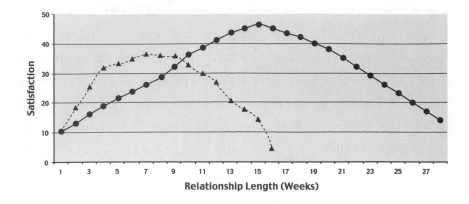

I sometimes think about this like food. Imagine that you eat a glazed doughnut with chocolate frosting. When you eat a doughnut, you feel good right off the bat. You get a sugar rush, and it is so tasty that you want to have three more. After twenty minutes or so, however, the sugar leaves your system and you start to feel sluggish and cranky. You then have to eat another doughnut or (my personal favorite) drink a cup of coffee to bring back the excitement.

Now, imagine that you eat a salad with some chicken. There is no rush, no excitement, and no burst of sugary goodness; however, after twenty minutes you feel pretty good. You don't crash and you don't need to drink the coffee.

Narcissists can be like eating doughnuts. Lots of taste, but little in the way of nourishment. What would this look like in relationships terms? Well, the taste of sugar may be likened to excitement, the rush that you get in a new relationship with a narcissist. Nourishment in a relationship, however, is more like intimacy. The experience of getting to know and trust someone you care about and who cares about you. We actually looked at excitement and intimacy in our graphs of relationships. The results were pretty powerful. Figure 2 shows the excitement in relationships with narcissists. (To make the differences more clear, I adjusted the relationships with the narcissists and non-narcissists so that they had the same length. In reality, the relationships with the narcissists were shorter.) What is clear is that relationships with narcissists (the dashed line with triangles) are more exciting during the initial stages than relationships with non-narcissists. Dating narcissists can clearly be exciting.

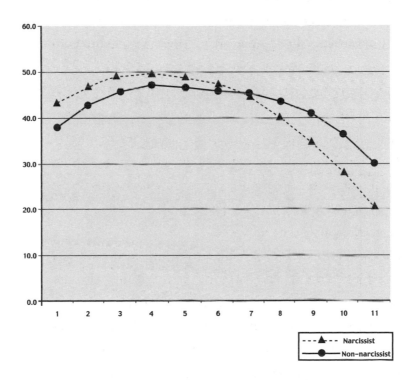

What is missing from relationships with narcissists? Figure 3 maps intimacy across the relationship. What is clear is that relationships with narcissists (the dashed line with triangles) do not have nearly the level of intimacy that relationships with non-narcissists do. It can be exciting dating narcissists, but the intimacy that is necessary to nourish a strong relationship is missing.

To summarize, relationships with narcissists may be initially satisfying, but the satisfaction drops off quickly and hard. In the same way that eating glazed doughnuts gives you a rush but offers little in the way of nourishment, relationships with narcissists can be exciting but offer little in the way of intimacy. To make matters worse, the drop in satisfaction that comes with the experience of dating narcissists doesn't end when the relationship ends.

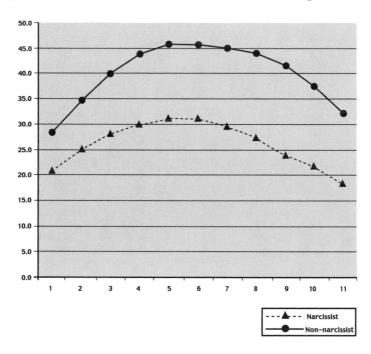

The Double Curse of Dating Narcissists

Narcissists make bad relationship partners in the long run, and, unfortunately, the psychological turmoil does not stop even after the relationship ends and the narcissistic partner disappears. I think about this as the double curse of dating narcissists. The first is the problems in the relationship and the second is the difficulty in emotionally getting over the relationship after it is over in reality. Relationships with narcissists can haunt women, sometimes for years. Women have a tendency to dwell on these relationships. They tend to think obsessively about their narcissistic ex-partners. They think about what happened, what went wrong, and what could have been. (Psychologists sometimes use the word *rumination* to describe the repetitive thinking about a topic.) They keep trying to explain the narcissist's behaviors: How could someone I loved be such a jerk? This type of thinking about the past is not fun. It is usually accompanied by negative feelings like anxiety, worry, or depression. Even worse, it interferes with starting new relationships. It is difficult to start a new relationship when you still spend time every day thinking about some narcissist you met. Women sometimes even think that there is something wrong with them because they can't get the relationship out of their minds. Even worse, they may think that there was something special or magical about the past relationship—Why would I keep thinking about it if it weren't special and important? Don't you only obsess about people whom you really love?

The truth is that this obsession on a past relationship with a narcissist has less to do with the importance of the relationship with the narcissist, and more to do with the seeming inconsistency and irrationality of the narcissists' behavior. When things don't make sense, we remember them better, think about them more, and find them harder to forget. These psychological processes are not limited to dating narcissists; they are very simple processes that happen all the time.

Here is an example of a basic memory process that I use in my class. Start out by imagining a guy named Mike. *Mike is a nice guy*. Now I am going to list some of Mike's behaviors:

1. Mike bought his girlfriend flowers.
2. Mike helps old ladies cross the street.
3. Mike donates money to charity.
4. Mike killed his cat.
5. Mike volunteers to help the homeless.
6. Mike dressed up as Santa Claus at Christmas.

After reading this list, what do you remember about Mike? If you are like most people, what you remember is that Mike killed his cat. Why? This doesn't make sense, because the cat killing doesn't fit with your image of Mike. As soon as you read that Mike, the nice guy, killed his cat, you start asking why. This is a natural thing to do—Mike's niceness and cat killing seem inconsistent, and this inconsistency needs to be resolved.

When I give this example in class, students always come up with some resolution to the cat killing. Some of the students change their opinion of Mike. They say that he really isn't a nice guy. Instead, he is a sociopath that acts nice on the surface, but is cold-hearted on the inside. Other students, however, make excuses for Mike. Some say that Mike killed his cat by accident, usually by backing out over her in the driveway. Others say that Mike euthanized his cat because she was sick; he had to put the cat out of her misery. Whatever the conclusions, the inconsistency in Mike's behavior makes it hard to forget about.

The same process is true about the behavior of narcissists. All you need to do is change some of the behaviors of Mike the narcissist.

1. Mike loves me.
2. Mike bought me flowers.
3. Mike has lots of friends.
4. Mike hit on my sister.
5. Mike volunteers to help the homeless.
6. Mike dressed up as Santa Claus at Christmas.

One of those behaviors didn't make sense, and thus will be ruminated on until it does.

Of course, if understanding the inconsistent behavior of a narcissistic boyfriend was purely an intellectual exercise, it would be difficult, but not too difficult, to figure out. Your friends, for example, probably would have a pretty easy time figuring out the behavior of your narcissistic boyfriend. They would say he was a jerk who put on a false front. End of story.

It is much tougher for the woman in the relationship, however, because the issues become very personal. They have to do with the woman's belief in herself. When such self-belief processes become involved, a psychological process called "cognitive dissonance" can kick in. This is a process by which we rationalize our beliefs and behaviors. An easy example of cognitive dissonance can be seen in smoking. We all know that smoking is very dangerous and likely to kill us in the long run, yet many people still choose to smoke. This leads to a large inconsistency, which makes us feel anxious or guilty and which needs to be resolved. This resolution can take several forms. I will address these in order.[11]

To start with, you have the two inconsistent beliefs:

1. I smoke.
2. Smoking kills.

Thinking about this inconsistency is uncomfortable, so what can we do? First, we can change one of the beliefs. We can quit smoking, or we can say that smoking doesn't kill. This is straightforward, but also difficult, because we like smoking, and we know that smoking kills. Fortunately, there are other ways to rationalize our inconsistent beliefs. One way is to add another belief that will make the others consistent. For example, we can say things like, "but I exercise," or "but I eat healthy foods," or (my personal favorite) "I only smoke when I drink," or "something else will kill me first." A final technique is just to say that things don't matter. If they don't matter, they won't cause us to become upset. High school kids do this by saying thing like, "I don't care if smoking kills me—I didn't ask to be born!" All of these rationalizations will work for a short while, but they are so weak and transparent that it is hard for them to last for a long time.

We use similar rationalizations with relationships. Imagine the beliefs:

1. I loved Mike.
2. Mike was a narcissistic jerk.

This is tough to reconcile. You can change one of the beliefs, "I never really loved Mike," but that is tough because it isn't true and it means that you can't trust your feelings. You can also deny the fact that Mike was a jerk. This would make you feel better in the short run, but who wants to spend their life in denial? You can also rationalize by adding a range of other beliefs. You can say, for example, "Mike didn't mean to be a narcissistic jerk; he had a bad childhood," or "Mike was just misunderstood." These will make you feel better in the short run, but are not the healthiest. They are also false. Likewise, you can say things such as "Mike misled me" or "I didn't see Mike for who he was." This is probably the truth, but it is hard to believe because it brings on more dissonance. Basically, you are admitting that you were manipulated. Nobody feels good admitting they were taken advantage of; instead, you feel stupid. But it is better to admit that than to make up some silly excuse for Mike and his lousy behavior. Furthermore, after learning about narcissists' skills in starting relationships, you shouldn't feel stupid. It happens to most people.

The final simple reason for the difficulty in forgetting relationships with narcissists is that we often make the mistake of *trying* to forget, rather than just moving on. The problem with trying to forget can be seen with a simple example that psychologists have used for years:[12]

Try not to think about a white bear for the next two minutes.

What happens when you try this? Well, at first you might intentionally think of something else. When you do that, you don't think about the white bear. But then you check yourself to make sure that you aren't thinking about the white bear. It might go something like, "Okay, I'm thinking about my schedule tomorrow, I'm definitely not thinking about a white bear. Oops, I just thought about the white bear...." The white bear doesn't go away. It keeps intruding into your thoughts as long as you try to forget it. The secret to not thinking about a white bear is not to try to not think about it. Just move on, your thoughts will naturally turn to other things and the white bear will pop into your head less and less frequently.

The same is true for past relationship partners. If you try not to think about them, you will keep thinking about them. Imagine waking up every day and saying, "Today I will not think about Mike." You've already thought about Mike. Then, at the end of the day, when you check to make sure that you didn't think about Mike, you think about Mike again. That is twice in one day—and that is on a good day! The better solution is to acknowledge that it is natural to think about Mike from time to time, and then get on with your life. Mike will keep appearing, but these appearances will get less and less frequent.

To summarize, narcissists can cause psychological suffering even after the relationship ends. This does not mean that you are crazy, or that the relationship with the narcissists was somehow special or important. Instead, it can be explained by some very simple psychological processes. The reason that narcissists are so hard to forget is that their behavior seems to make no sense from the perspective of the person in love with them. Trying to forget the person can sometimes make things worse. The key is trying to get a realistic perspective on the narcissistic partner, and then to move on.

Chapter Four

What Can You Do About It?

In the first three chapters of this book I presented a portrait of narcissists, discussed how narcissists approach romantic relationships, and described why women can be attracted to narcissists. I hope that you have gained some insight into narcissists' behavior and that this will have some positive impact on your life. In this chapter I venture a little more directly into the self-help realm. I want to discuss some of the ways in which women can cope with narcissistic men. How do you avoid dating them? What can you do if you are dating them? I present some thoughts, suggestions, and tools. I hope that these can go a long way in helping to ease the pain of relationships with narcissistic men.

Don't Do It—It's a Trap!

My first suggestion is guaranteed to be the most effective. If you do not want to date narcissistic men, do your best to avoid them. This sounds simple—it is simple—but it is the step in self-control efforts that most people skip. In order to explain this, let me digress for a moment into the topic of dieting. Dieting is an area where we all struggle with self-control, so it is a good place to discuss self-control principles.

There is a truism in dieting: If you do not want to eat chocolate cake, do not buy it at the supermarket and do not leave it in your fridge. Do not even walk by the bakery at the market. Why? It is relatively easy to avoid chocolate cake if it is not around. As the saying goes, "out of sight, out of mind." You might think about the chocolate cake occasionally while you are sitting at home. Perhaps you will see a commercial or a scene on TV where people are eating cake and think to yourself, "chocolate cake would be so good right now." But, if you do not have the cake in your kitchen, you are unlikely to get in the car, drive to the market to buy it, bring it home, and eat it. The thoughts of the cake will come and then they will go.

Now imagine a different situation. You do not avoid the cake. Instead, you buy the big chocolate cake and put it in your fridge. You decide that you will save it for the weekend and then just have one slice. This sounds like a great plan and you are sure that you can resist until Friday. On Tuesday night you come home and open the fridge to make a salad. There is the cake. You start thinking about cake and use your willpower to resist. You eat your salad, but afterwards you think about the cake again. Still, you remain steadfast and feel pretty proud of yourself. The next day the same things happen. You get your glass of orange juice in the morning and see the cake. It does not sound great right then, but at lunch at the office the image of the cake pops into your head. Somehow, your salad does not taste so good. That night you vow not to have the cake again. It looks even more tempting than last night, but you still resist. Again, your willpower triumphs!

The next day the process repeats itself. Unfortunately, you have a bad day at work. One of the clients yells at you and your manager does not take your side of the argument. By the time you get home you are angry and exhausted. You go to make dinner and again see the cake sitting there. You say to yourself, "I'll just have a little bit of frosting." You do and it is so good. You then wrap the cake back up and say that you will save the rest. You make it through dinner and start thinking about the cake again. You decide to just have a little piece to clean up the now messy frosting. The cake tastes great. You then realize that you have blown your whole diet plan. This makes you feel even more depressed than you already did when you came home. You say to yourself, "What the Hell. I already broke my diet, so I might as well go for it." You manage to eat half the cake and you feel great— for about ten minutes. Unfortunately, the next day you feel guilty and fat. You do not know why you ate the cake and you throw the remainder away. You are even more depressed than when you started.[1]

There are several morals to this story:

1. *Avoidance is best.* If you had just avoided buying the cake in the first place, you could have avoided the entire fiasco. You would not have had to think about the cake all week, your lunch would have tasted better, you would not have binged, and you would not feel depressed and guilty. It only takes a

little bit of willpower to avoid things; it takes a lot of willpower to resist temptations that are right in front of you.

2. *Human willpower is terribly weak.* We all have great intentions. We want to eat healthy meals, exercise and work diligently, and not get in arguments with our friends or partners. We know that doing these things will only serve to benefit our lives in the long run. However, we are often unsuccessful in our pursuits. We eat junk, are lazy, and are nasty to those whom we care about.

3. *Willpower is at its weakest when we are tired, stressed, or otherwise mentally depleted.* When we feel well rested and happy, we can vow to do all sorts of great things. When we get tired and stressed, however, these promises that we made to ourselves often go out the window.

What does this have to do with dating narcissists? Think of narcissists as chocolate cake. Chocolate cake looks good. It gives you a rush when you eat it. Sometimes your cheeks flush and your brain secretes chemicals that mimic those of love. The problem with chocolate cake is that the day after you go for it, you feel sick, you feel sluggish, and you gain weight. Chocolate cake can be fun in the short term, but is damaging in the long term. The same is true of relationships with narcissists. He looks good. You may be attracted to him right away. He can be exciting to date— it might even feel like love. Unfortunately, the fun and excitement only last a short while. Relationships with narcissists ultimately can hurt your sense of self and damage your future relationships. Dating narcissists is tempting, but it is best to be avoided.

You can avoid relationships with narcissistic men the same way you avoid chocolate cake. If at all possible, do not date narcissistic men. Period. Do not spend time with them and think, "It is okay, I just won't get involved." Do not think "He will change" or "He is really a good guy inside" or "He may be arrogant with all the other people in his life, but he really cares about me" or "Hey, it is just for fun, I won't get in too deep and therefore won't get hurt" or "He's Mr. Right Now." Just avoid the situation.

Basically, it is much easier to avoid the narcissist all together than it is to flirt and play at getting involved. Once you start getting involved, the rationalization starts and you are at risk for getting more and more deeply involved.

Of course, you may be thinking, "Sure, it sounds easy to avoid narcissistic men, but narcissists are not like chocolate cake. Chocolate cake does not disguise itself as tofu in order to sneak onto your plate. Narcissistic men, however, act like something they are not in order to start a relationship. So how do I avoid them?"

I agree completely with the sentiment. Often you do know that a man is a narcissist. Maybe you have seen how he treats other women or maybe he has obvious narcissistic traits. Many times, however, narcissistic men hide their true intentions. So, what do you look for in order to spot a narcissist? I have compiled a list of potential warnings signs. This is neither a perfect nor a complete list, but it is a good start. I present two types of warning signs.

First, there are the behavioral warning signs. These are the easy ones that most people pay attention to. I then present warning signs in the physical and social environment. These are subtler and often overlooked, but they are important when identifying narcissists.

Specific behavioral warning signs. Sometimes all you have to go on when judging a man is how he behaves with you. Here is a partial list of behavioral warning signs. There is no secret formula to use (e.g., three out of five does not necessarily mean that the man is a narcissist). Instead, if you see several of these behaviors, you might want to keep your guard up a bit and look for additional evidence.

- He talks about himself and his achievements constantly. The conversation always turns out to be about him.
- He has an extremely positive opinion of his intelligence and skills.
- He twists things so that he ends up looking good.
- He thinks that he is highly attractive. He spends more time in front of the mirror than you do.
- There was a sense of immediate attraction or excitement when you first met. This is not always bad, of course, just keep your eyes open.
- He puts other people down quite a bit. This is how he makes himself feel good.
- There is charm overkill. You sometimes get this feeling from salesmen. You know that it is an act.

- He does not seem very interested in forming a caring or committed relationship with you (or anyone).
- He desires to associate with highly popular people rather than close friends.
- He loves to be the center of attention.
- Narcissists are prone to be unfaithful. They also are good at making excuses. Remember, if he is cheating on someone else by being with you, he is likely to cheat on you as well.
- He reacts to criticisms or slights with angry outbursts. He often sees criticisms where none are intended.
- There is evidence of violent or abusive behavior.
- He is materialistic. He enjoys material possessions that make him look popular and important (brand name clothes, jewelry, cars, etc.).
- He expresses a large sense of entitlement.

There are also warning signs from the social or physical environment. These include the following.

Location, location, location. The first warning sign has to do with location. People often get so focused on "reading people" that they forget to pay attention to their social situation. Great white sharks live near colonies of sea lions. If you want to avoid great white sharks, avoid sea lions. Wolves live near herds of caribou. If you want to avoid wolves, avoid caribou herds. Narcissists thrive in unstable social environments where looks and first impressions really matter. When you are in these types of environments, be on the lookout. Examples of these environments are bars (especially those that are known as pick-up places), parties where most of the people are strangers, and big cities.

Watch how men behave with "inferiors" and strangers. Narcissists can hide their personality relatively easily when first meeting a woman. They can put out the charm and act like nice, successful guys. These narcissistic men, however, are not likely to use these techniques with people they are not trying to manipulate. Watch how these men treat "underlings." Are they decent and respectful or are they nasty and likely to act in an overtly superior way? If a man whom you have recently started seeing treats you with charm and treats others dismissively, that should set off warning bells.

Listen to others' impressions. How many times have you seen your friends in a relationship with a bad guy? You might say something to your friend, but she may dismiss everything that you say. She might even stop speaking with you in order to keep the relationship. The reason, of course, is that all of us can have highly distorted views of our dating partners (and this is not necessarily bad). If you are interested in a guy who you have concerns about, you might want to ask for your friends' opinions. You may ask them to be honest and actually listen to what they say. Yes, this can be tough.

Find out how men behave in past relationships. Many men will have a reputation earned in their past romantic relationships. Perhaps they have a history of hurting women. Perhaps they have a history of good relationships. Pay attention to the history. Yes, there are two sides to every story, so history can be difficult to judge. Still, if there is a pattern of bad relationships where the man has earned the reputation of a "player" or a "self-centered SOB," there may be a real problem. Sometimes, where there is smoke, there is fire. There is a truism in the study of personality that says past behavior is the best predictor of future behavior. Bottom line: get a dating résumé.

To summarize, the easiest way to avoid getting involved with narcissists is to stay away. If you start spending time with a narcissistic man, there is a major risk that you will start up a relationship. Willpower is not all that it is cracked up to be.

Of course, it is often difficult to distinguish a narcissist from a decent guy. Narcissists are skilled at putting on a good act to avoid detection. Sometimes it is best to judge a guy by how he behaves with people other than yourself, how he treats those beneath him, etc. Likewise, it is good to get input from friends and others. There are also several behavioral warning signs that may clue you in to narcissism. None of these signs are perfect, but if you see one after the other, it may be good to avoid the relationship. We will discuss some of these in the next section.

Have I Done It? Analyzing Your Relationship

In the previous section, we discussed some strategies for identifying narcissists *before* becoming involved in a relationship. In this section, I will describe some specific techniques for analyzing your current and past relationships to see if you are or have been involved with a narcissistic man. These techniques are derived from psychological research on narcissism and include: writing and analyzing a relationship story, drawing a relationship graph, and taking a relationship quiz.

A Relationship Story

The relationship story is a technique that we have often used in our research on narcissism. I described some of this research earlier. What I would recommend is to write three stories. I would begin by writing two stories about past relationships. Ideally, you can think about your relationships with two people, one who was narcissistic, and one who was not narcissistic. (If you don't have two past relationships like this, it would still be useful to write about someone else's relationship that you know well.) I will give you some guidelines below to help you with this. The point of this exercise is to help you see the important differences between narcissists and nice guys. The instructions for the narcissistic story are as follows:[2]

Please tell a story from your life in which you dated or became involved romantically with a highly narcissistic or self-centered person. The relationship that you write about should have occurred in the past.

Who is a narcissistic or self-centered person? This person would have had several characteristics. He would have had a very high opinion of himself and have acted in an arrogant or conceited manner. He may have thought or talked about fame or success. He may have also thought that he was "special" and was only willing to associate with other special persons or groups. He may have needed admiration and felt entitled to special treatment, perhaps taking advantage of other people. He may have been envious of other persons, or thought that others were envious of him. He may have lacked empathy or caring.

You may not have dated anyone exactly like this. If so, please think about someone whom you have dated who has at least some of these characteristics.

The instructions for the non-narcissist story are the mirror image of the above:

Please tell a true story from your life in which you dated or became involved romantically with a person who was not at all narcissistic or self-centered. The relationship that you write about should have occurred in the past.

Who is *not* a narcissistic or self-centered person? This person would have lacked several characteristics. He would *not* have had a very high opinion of himself or have acted in an arrogant or conceited manner. He may *not* have thought or talked about fame or success. He may also *not* have thought that he was "special" and was *not* only willing to associate with other special persons or groups. He would *not* have needed admiration and felt entitled to special treatment, and would *not* have taken advantage of other people. He may *not* have been envious of other persons, or thought that others were envious of him. He would have been empathetic and caring.

You may not have dated anyone like this. If so, please think about someone who you have dated that has at least some of these characteristics.

In order to get an accurate story about both partners, it is not necessary to write many pages. However, it is useful to focus on:

- reasons that you were attracted to him,
- the best parts of the relationship,
- the worst parts of the relationship, and
- why the relationship ended.

Analyzing the stories. The analysis of these stories is relatively simple. All you do is look for certain themes or behaviors in each one. It is best if you try to pretend that you are an outside observer or scientist analyzing these stories. That way, your own feelings are less likely to interfere with the results.

What themes or behaviors do you look for? Well, you will certainly see some patterns just reading through the stories. Some of these may be very relevant to your life, and are important to pay attention to. There are also behaviors that we find in many (although not all) of these stories, and these may be worth looking for. To make it easier, I have included a coding sheet below. All you need to do is check whether one of these traits or behaviors was part of your relationship ("yes"), or wasn't ("no"). The first three "yes" responses (the first numbers 1–3 below) are typically what we find in relationships with non-narcissists. For example, the non-narcissists tend to be kind, caring, and considerate. The rest of the items are all more common in relationships with narcissists. When you are done coding your stories, what you should see is that in the stories about the narcissistic partners you have checked "yes" many more times—except on the first three items.

What attracted you to the relationship and what was the best part of the relationship?

_____

_____

_____

1. We had emotional intimacy;
   we were close friends   Yes __ No __

2. He was kind/caring/considerate   Yes __ No __

3. He was sensitive/a good listener   Yes __ No __

4. He was ambitious   Yes __ No __

5. He was confident and extroverted   Yes __ No __

6. He was popular and had high social status   Yes __ No __

7. He was charming   Yes __ No __

8. We had an immediate attraction   Yes __ No __

9. We had an exciting relationship   Yes __ No __

What was the worst part of the relationship?

_____

_____

_____

1. He was vain about his looks   Yes __ No __

2. He was self-centered and talked about himself Yes __ No __

3. He put other people down   Yes __ No __

4. He was arrogant/cocky   Yes __ No __

5. He ignored me   Yes __ No __

6. He was unfaithful   Yes __ No __

7. He lied   Yes __ No __

8. He played games in the relationship   Yes __ No __

9. He flirted with others   Yes __ No __

10. He needed to be the center of attention   Yes __ No __

11. He was controlling   Yes __ No __

12. He was manipulative   Yes __ No __

13. He was violent/aggressive   Yes __ No __

14. He considered me to be a trophy   Yes __ No __

15. He was materialistic   Yes __ No __

16. His private personality was different
    from his public personality   Yes __ No __

17. Things were always my fault   Yes __ No __

A story about your current relationship. Coding stories about past relationships should have given you some insight into the differences between relationships with narcissists and non-narcissists. Now, the task becomes one of analyzing your current relationship. This can be done in exactly the same way. Simply write a story about your relationship, paying particular attention to what attracted you to your partner, and what were the best and worst parts of your relationship.

Once you are done with the story, you can code it with the same coding form that you used before. Here is the big question: Does your relationship look like a relationship with a narcissist or with a non-narcissist? You can tell this by comparing your current relationship with those in the past.

A Relationship Graph

The relationship graph gets at the same idea as the story, but uses a graphic representation of the relationship. This technique works very well for past relationships, and also may give you some insight into a current relationship. We saw some of the results of these relationships graphs in the last chapter.

In order to analyze a relationship, I suggest drawing three graphs. The first is about your overall satisfaction in the relationship, the second is about the emotional intimacy in the relationship, and the third is about the excitement in the relationship.[3] All you need for the graph is a box with two labels.

The box below is for satisfaction. You can do similar graphs for intimacy and excitement. To use the graph, draw a line across that represents how satisfied you were across the course of the relationship. The exact dates don't matter; it is the pattern of satisfaction that does.

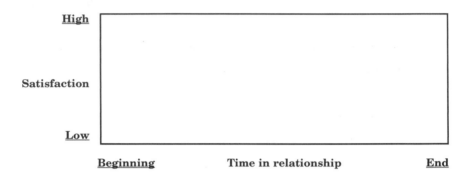

What do you do with the graphs? The key is the pattern of changes in the three graphs. As we saw in the last chapter, the pattern with relationships with narcissists is one where satisfaction and excitement spike up at the beginning, and then drop quickly. Intimacy, however, never gets that high. In contrast, in relationships with non-narcissists, the satisfaction and excitement may rise more slowly, but the intimacy will rise as well. The more you get to know the person, the closer and more satisfied you become.

A Relationship Quiz

Taking a quiz about a current or past relationship is also an effective way to analyze it. This is similar to the relationship story, but is easier to do. In the quiz below, simply put a check mark by the items that best reflect your relationship. The quiz is phrased for a past relationship, but it is easy to use for a current relationship as well.

Which of these traits led you to be initially attracted to your partner (check all that apply)?

1. ____ Physical appearance
2. ____ Confidence
3. ____ Ambition and social status
4. ____ Charm
5. ____ Wealth or material possessions
6. ____ Popularity
7. ____ High social status

Which of these statements describe how your partner acted in the relationship most of the time? (check all that apply)

8. ____ He was materialistic
9. ____ He was not a good listener
10. ____ He treated me like a "trophy"
11. ____ He was sexually unfaithful
12. ____ He didn't always seem very committed to the relationship

13. ____ He often put me down or criticized me

14. ____ He was over-controlling

15. ____ He was manipulative

16. ____ He frequently ignored me

17. ____ He was aggressive toward me

18. ____ He flirted with others

19. ____ He lied to me on several occasions

20. ____ He was different in private than in public

21. ____ He "played games" in the relationship

22. ____ He pressured me sexually

Which of these statements describe how your relationship was most of the time? (check all that apply)

23. ____ We had a very physical relationship

24. ____ We had a very "unhealthy" relationship

Scoring the scale: Give yourself 1 point for every checkmark. Your total score can range from 0 to 24. A score of 0 indicates a very non-narcissistic relationship; a score of 24 is a very narcissistic relationship. Any score of 10 or above suggests that this could be a narcissistic partner.

The relationship stories, graphs, and quiz offer three different ways to analyze your relationship. My feeling is that it is useful to use all three of these techniques. In addition, I think that it is very important to analyze positive relationships with nice people. The relationships with the narcissists will stand in stark contrast to other, healthier relationships. Seeing this difference in black and white will aid in your understanding.

So, what do you do if you find out that your boyfriend has all the hallmarks of a narcissist? You might not want to leave the relationship, but you don't want to stay committed to an arrogant jerk either. Can you change a narcissist into a nice guy? We will tackle this topic in the next section.

Okay, I've Done It—Can Narcissists Change?

You find yourself in a relationship with a narcissist. You did not set out to date a narcissistic man, but you are doing so nonetheless. Maybe you have invested a lot of time or energy in the relationship or maybe there are parts of the relationship that you like or maybe you do not think that there are any other possible relationships out there or maybe you do not want to be a "quitter." Whatever the reason, you might want to stay in the relationship. At the same time, you know that things would be better if only your partner was not a narcissist and didn't act like a jerk. The logical next step, of course, would be to change your partner's personality. If only you could get rid of the narcissistic, self-centered aspects of the man you're dating, he would be a pretty nice guy. In this section I want to discuss the reasonableness of this course of action. I begin by addressing the possibility of changing severe narcissism or narcissistic personality disorder. This type of pathological narcissism can cause the most relationship problems, and it is also the most difficult to change.

"People never change," "do not count on anybody changing," or some variant of these statements is often heard in discussions of relationships. Many people go through life with the message that individuals cannot change. The good news is that this statement is false. Many people change throughout the course of their lives. People can develop better work habits, learn to eat healthy foods, develop an optimistic outlook on life, and acquire a range of relationship skills. People can change.

The little-bit-less-than-good news is that change is difficult. Take for example the desire to "get in shape." Many people want to be physically fit. This is not surprising because there are many benefits to being physically fit. Being fit will lessen the chance for getting many health problems, increase feelings of happiness and well-being, and improve physical attractiveness. People also know how to get fit. They need to eat healthier food and exercise. This is not rocket science—the vast majority of people know how to do this reasonably well. Unfortunately, very few Americans get and stay physically fit. They say they are too busy to exercise, they do not have time to eat well, they keep trying largely ineffective diets, or they say that they will start as their New Year's resolution. The message is that even when people want to change, they do not always do it. Sometimes it even takes a heart attack or other health crisis to get people to exercise! Change is possible, but change is tough. You must desire to change, know the steps to take in order to change, and act on your knowledge and desire. Breakdowns can occur at all three of these points.

The semi-bad news is that in the world of psychological functioning, all things are difficult to change, but some things are more difficult to change than others. The well-respected clinical psychologist

Martin Seligman wrote a book outlining these differences. At the "easier to change" end of the spectrum are psychological problems that have a large learning component and seem like "difficulties." Phobias or irrational fears are a very good example of this. Many people have phobias to different objects or situations. Some of the more common phobias are the fear of public speaking, snakes, or flying.[4]

More difficult to change are what psychologists call "Axis I" disorders. These are what we often think of as "mental illnesses." They often seem to strike the person like any other illness. They have specific symptoms and there are several available treatments. One of the more common disorders, for example, is depression. Depression can strike almost any normal person. The cause may be a romantic loss, a hormonal fluctuation, or some unidentified factor. The symptoms include sad mood, lack of energy, changes in appetite, sleep disturbance (too much or too little sleep), low self-esteem, etc. Sometimes depression will go away of its own accord. The loss of a loved one, for example, will often lead to depression, and this will dissipate with time and the grieving process. There are several effective treatments for depression. The most effective is a combination of cognitive-behavioral therapy and anti-depressant medication (e.g., Prozac). Many people get depressed and most get through it and go back to being their old selves.

Another group of disorders that are also somewhat difficult to change are addictions to narcotics, gambling, etc. Alcoholism, for example, is still extremely prevalent in this country. Alcoholics can change, but it is difficult. The best guess is that about a third of alcoholics manage to stay sober for a long period of time, another third learn to drink normally throughout their lives, and another third never recover and may have miserable and shortened lives as a result. One of the groups that appears to be effective at changing alcoholics is Alcoholics Anonymous. (I say "appears" because there are not really good numbers on success rates and individuals in AA are not supposed to boast publicly about their successful recovery.) If you attend an AA meeting, you will hear many stories about people quitting drinking. Most of the stories go something like this: I was drinking too much. It was ruining the lives of people around me and I was too selfish to notice. Finally something really bad happened (my family left, I went to jail, I was living in my car, etc.) and I hit rock bottom. I then made an effort to quit drinking. It has taken a considerable effort, but I now feel better and I know in my heart that if I kept drinking I would be dead, crazy, or in jail.

Notice what alcoholics do *not* say: My girlfriend or wife wanted me to quit drinking, so I did. Often people need to suffer a great deal before they quit drinking.

So, are there aspects of psychological functioning that are even more difficult to change than depression or alcoholism? The answer is yes. Aspects of an individual's character—psychologists call these Axis II or personality disorders—are extremely resistant to change. This list of disorders includes borderline personality disorder and antisocial personality disorder. All of these disorders are tough because they are part of who the individual *is*. Unlike depression or alcoholism, they are not an illness or problem that the individuals can just remove. Still, even people with these personality disorders can sometimes change given the desire to change, a really talented clinician, and time.

As you may have suspected, the bad news is that narcissism falls into this category. Narcissism reflects an individual's entire character of personality. Narcissism is not a mental illness or a bad habit—it is a way of life. Still, narcissism can be changed, given the situation I just described: a desire to change, a talented clinician, and time.

The really bad news is that narcissists very, very rarely want to change. *Narcissists like being narcissists.* Repeat: narcissists like being narcissists. Imagine that you thought that you were more talented than everyone else, great looking, and charming. You spent all your energy on yourself and did not really want to be in a close relationship with another person. Would you want to change? Of course not! Everyone else should change to realize your special nature, but there would be absolutely no reason on earth for you to change.

Only on rare occasions will narcissists want to change. One experience that may drive narcissists to seek therapy is depression following a string of failures. This does not happen often because narcissists are experts at rationalizing away their failures by blaming others. When a narcissist cannot succeed for an extended period of time, however, depression may arise. A narcissist's goal at this time is to get some positive feedback and adoration. If he gets this in therapy, the depression will go away. Unfortunately, the narcissism will also return.

Narcissists may also enter couples' therapy. For example, a wife might convince her narcissistic husband to get relationship counseling. The husband may go, but his goal will not be to change his positive self-image. He may just want his wife to change!

Narcissists may also enter therapy so that they can tell their friends that they are seeing a famous therapist. The psychiatrist James Masterson tells an amusing story about this. His practice, which specializes in treating narcissists, was written about in the *New York Times*. The next week, several narcissists made appointments for treatment. They all knew that they were narcissists and wanted to see a famous therapist. Dr. Masterson told each of them that were indeed suffering from narcissistic personality disorder. He then told them that although he could not take on any new clients at the time, he would set them up with one of his skilled colleagues. Not one of the narcissists wanted an appointment. Clearly, the narcissists' goal in therapy was not to change, but instead to gain social status by seeing a famous New York psychiatrist![5]

Now, imagine that there is the rare narcissist who truly wants to change his character. The really, really bad news is that even in this circumstance, it may be quite difficult. Clinicians who work with narcissistic individuals need to be extremely talented. Narcissists are good at charming and manipulating clinicians just as they are good at manipulating everyone else. Furthermore, there are very few effective treatments for narcissism. We know that phobias can be cured with progressive desensitization. We know that depression can be cured with a combination of cognitive-behavioral therapy and anti-depressants. There are no "miracle" cures for narcissism. Pills have no effect. Therapists who take on narcissistic clients (and many simply will not) generally rely on some form of psychodynamic therapy or a complex form of cognitive-behavioral therapy. This can work, but it relies heavily on a clinician's skill. This type of therapy is far more difficult than basic behavioral therapy and also far less certain in its outcome.

Finally, the really, really, really bad news is that therapy for narcissism done with a talented therapist and a willing client can take *years* to work. It cannot be done in a week or a month and often not in a year. It is very, very difficult and time consuming in the best of cases.

Let us sum up what we have just discussed. People can change, but it is difficult. Often there needs to be a strong desire to change (e.g., a heart attack may finally get someone to exercise, or a car wreck might get someone to stop drinking). Certain psychological issues can be changed relatively easily, such as phobias. Others, such as depression, can be addressed, but it takes some time and effort. Narcissism, however, reflects the basic workings of someone's personality and is thus more difficult to change. This is complicated by the fact that *narcissists do not want to change because they are special and wonderful people who expect the rest of the world to change for them.* Even if a narcissist does want to change, skilled psychologists and psychiatrists have tremendous difficulty helping the change process. Many simply will not treat narcissists. Finally, even when a willing narcissist gets together with skilled clinicians, change can take years.

This leads us to the big question: Can you change your extremely narcissistic partner? The unfortunate answer is probably not.

Nobody wants to hear that they cannot change their partner, even though at some level they know that this is the truth. If you are in a relationship with someone with NPD, and (for whatever the reasons) want to stay, my advice would be to make sure that your partner is really willing to change and then seek some form of professional therapy. As I mentioned, there are two basic types of therapies used for narcissism: psychodynamic therapies and cognitive-behavioral therapies (interpersonal therapies, although less common, may also be useful). There is no good evidence that I can find supporting the success of any one type of therapy. My bias is usually toward the cognitive therapies, but much depends on the clinician.

It can be difficult to find talented clinicians, especially when it comes to treating personality disorders. One course of action that I suggest is to contact the psychology department of the nearest large research university. Many large cities have universities where they train clinical psychologists. These universities often will have a psychology clinic that can either offer therapy by people up-to-date on the latest techniques, or direct you to well-trained clinicians in your community. The other advantage is that these clinics often have sliding fee scales, so they can sometime be more affordable. There are no guarantees that therapy will work, but it is an option.

Fortunately, many people are not dealing with severe narcissism in a partner. Some are probably involved with narcissistic men who have many of the important traits associated with narcissism, but have not done anything bad enough to destroy the relationships. In these relationships, the good may equal or even outweigh the bad, and the hope is that the narcissism will become diminished and the relationship will improve. With this type of more moderate narcissism, there is some possibility of change. I say this with caution, and also with the belief that in the vast majority of cases, it is a mistake to wait for change. Nevertheless, there are two ways in which narcissism can change.

First, narcissism may decrease with age. This does not happen to everyone by any means, but it does happen to the average person. The biggest drop seems to occur between the ages of thirty and fifty. Nobody knows why this drop occurs. It may be related to natural developmental processes that make men focus more on families and society. It may be that men may just find it more difficult to be arrogant when they have risen as far as they will rise in society. It is easy to be a big deal in high school or college, but harder in the real world. It may also reflect hormonal changes like decreased testosterone. Whatever the reason, the gradual change seems to be there.[6]

Second, there is some preliminary and unpublished evidence that a subgroup of narcissists can become better relationship partners. This change is accompanied by an interesting psychological process. Those married narcissists who feel that their spouse brings out caring-oriented, relational aspects of their personalities actually grow more committed and faithful in relationships. For example, a narcissist who feels that his wife makes him feel warm and caring will become more committed to the relationship.

How does one get a narcissist to see himself as caring, kind, and warm? There really is no known answer to that question. The research is in the very early stages. As it stands, it seems that this change can happen, but the reasons it happens are not known.

So, can narcissists change? The answer seems to be a very, very qualified "yes." Narcissists can change in therapy, but this is very hard to do. Some narcissists also will change with maturity and in certain relationships.

The next question, of course, is: Can you make a narcissist change? The answer to that is pretty much a "no." Narcissists really like being narcissists. Even when they get depressed, the best way to make them feel better is to pump up their egos. They don't really care about others, so they typically won't change for someone else. Even if narcissists do want to change (which is very rare), there is no sure way to change. All in all, I wouldn't place my bets on narcissists changing.

So, Should I Stay or Should I Go?

You are currently in a relationship with a narcissist. After reading the last section, you have concluded that you are unlikely to change a narcissist's character. The next question that you probably want to answer for yourself involves staying in the relationship. Is it best to try to make things work in the current relationship, get involved with someone else, or simply stay out of the relationship game for a while?

There is no easy answer to this question. The best thing to do is try to systematically think through your current situation and then decide. What I would like to do in this section is present a structured way to think about your relationship. This approach is based on the research of Professor Rusbult described in chapter two. According to this approach, there are three factors that lead to the decision to stay in a relationship. These are (a) your level of satisfaction in the relationship, (b) your investments in the relationship, and (c) your alternatives to the relationship. People will stay in relationships if they have high satisfaction, high investments, and few alternatives. I will discuss each of these separately.

Satisfaction. Satisfaction refers to how much you think that you are getting out of the relationship. Overall satisfaction contains three parts. The first includes *rewards*. Does the relationship make you feel good about yourself? Do you enjoy doing things with your partner? Do you get social support or emotional intimacy from your relationship? All of these would entail rewards.

The second part of satisfaction is the *costs* associated with the relationship. Do you feel bad about yourself in the relationship? Is your partner abusive? Does your partner restrict your activities inside or outside of the relationship? All of these would be relationship costs.

The final part of satisfaction goes by the fancy name *comparison level*. This is essentially what you have come to expect in relationships. If you have been in three relationships with terrific guys, you will not be very satisfied dating a mediocre guy. If you have been in three abusive relationships, however, a mediocre guy may be very satisfying. We judge the people we are with based on our past experiences. If you expect *really* bad treatment, you will be satisfied with just plain bad treatment.

Taking these three elements together we can get a pretty good idea of relationship satisfaction. Satisfaction equals our rewards in the relationship minus the costs and compared to what we have come to expect. If we have lots of rewards, very few costs, and we do not expect a lot from a relationship, then we will be very satisfied. If we have few rewards, many costs, and expect a lot from our relationship, then we will not be satisfied. There is also the tricky situation where we have a few rewards, many costs, but expect to be treated terribly in our relationships. In this situation we will be satisfied with even a bad relationship—because we expect even worse.

In terms of staying in a relationship with a narcissist, it is important to identify the rewards, costs, and expectations in the relationship. If you are satisfied with a bad relationship because you expect even worse, this should give you pause. Likewise, if there are many rewards, and many costs, you should think about how many costs you are willing to shoulder. Does the bad out-weigh the good?

Hillary Clinton, for example, has probably stayed satisfied in a relationship with a chronically unfaithful man (big cost) because the relationship offered many rewards (political power, perhaps emotional connection). She was willing to make this trade-off to stay in the relationship. Some women would make the same choice; some would not. These are the things to think about when deciding to date a narcissistic man.

Investments. Investments are one of the trickier issues in the decision to stay committed in a relationship. People will be more likely to stay in a relationship if they have large investments. Investments include things like shared living arrangements, kids, combined bank accounts, shared friends, and time. You will hear people say things like: "No way am I giving up on this relationship—I have invested two years in it!"

"We are staying together for the kids"

"If we split up, I am going to need to find all new friends because all *our* friends are *his* friends."

It is important to note that people will stay in unsatisfying relationships because they have a great deal invested in these relationships. My feeling is that this is often a mistake. This is especially true when the investment is time. Think about it. An investment is something that you make in order to have a payoff. When you invest in a stock, for example, you expect to get back more than you put in. When you invest time in a relationship, you expect to get back more than you put in as well. When you invest in a stock and it loses value (and looks like it will never get better), the smart thing to do is sell it and move on. It was a bad investment. Yes, it hurts to lose money, but it is better than holding a bad stock for thirty years. Bad economic investments are made all the time. When this happens you try to learn something to avoid repeating the mistake in the future. Imagine that you bought stock in some goofy Internet company in 1999. Your MrSoapdish.com stock started at $100 a share and went to $120 a share. You thought you were going to be a millionaire!

Then, the stock dropped back to $100, and you were sure it would go up. Then it dropped to $80 a share, but you kept holding on because you couldn't bear to lose money. Then the stock kept dropping to sixty dollars, forty dollars, and twenty dollars a share. You kicked yourself for not bailing out earlier, but you still didn't want to lose. You figured this is as bad as it would get. Finally the stock slid all the way to zero, and you lost your entire investment. This would be awful, and you would vow never again to hold onto a losing stock.

The same should be true of relationships. If you invest in a relationship and it does not work out at all, the smart thing to do is break it off and try something else. Yes it hurts, but it hurts a lot less than it would if you broke it off a year or two or three later when it had gotten really bad.

There is an even bigger economic mistake that you can make. The dumbest mistake that you can make with a bad economic investment is to invest more. People do this sometimes in the hopes that they can make up for their original loss. Economists have a good term for this mistake. They call it "throwing good money after bad." People do this in their relationships as well. The longer they are in a relationship, the more time they feel that they have invested. This, in turn, makes it ever more difficult to leave the relationship. So they redouble their energy and spend even more time on the relationship in hopes of getting back their investment. Think of it as "throwing good time after bad." One of our research subjects gave a classic example of this.

Laura was dating a cute, but very narcissistic guy named Stan at the beginning of the fall semester. They dated for a few months and she started to get the inkling that something was wrong. Stan was fun to be with at parties, but didn't spend time with her during the week. She also heard that he had "approached" one of her friends, although she tried to convince herself that this was just innocent. Over Thanksgiving, she brought Stan to meet her parents. Stan was very charming. Laura started to think that the relationship could work out in the long run. During Christmas break, however, Stan went skiing with some friends and did not call. Laura heard that there were other women on the trip, but was not certain. After Christmas, Stan became more and more of a jerk. He would rarely pay attention to her unless he was drinking, and the rumors of other women kept surfacing. Laura was really dissatisfied with how the relationship was going, but she kept thinking that she had invested so much time in the relationship and even introduced Stan to her parents (who would ask about him every time they called). She decided to stick with the relationship to see if she could make it work. Stan distanced himself more and more, and Laura kept investing more and more time and effort in trying to keep the relationship alive. That summer Stan went out West and Laura finally gave up. She realized that she had wasted a whole year in a losing relationship instead of breaking it off after the first couple months and looking for someone better. She also vowed not to make the same mistake in the future.

Many times I have had women tell me that the reason that they stayed with narcissistic men was because of the investment. They hated to give up the relationship because they had invested so much time in it, they would have to buy new furniture, or get a new apartment. From an outsider's perspective, these seem to be pretty weak reasons to stay in a bad relationship, but they are given all the time. My sense is that people get used to the bad relationship. They want to leave, but it just seems like such a waste. When they step back and look at the entire situation, they usually decide that the cost of leaving is worth it. Try looking at your relationship from the perspective of an observer. If it does not make sense, it may be time to stop throwing good time after bad.

There is one investment, however, that makes a decision to leave even an unsatisfying relationship with a narcissist very difficult: kids. When the investment that you lose by leaving a relationship is a stable family for your children, it may be worth staying in an unsatisfying relationship. Every situation, of course, is different. In general, however, it seems reasonable to suggest that intense effort should be made to make things work. Such efforts would include counseling with a psychologist, therapist, or religious representative (priest, rabbi, etc). Once you have a family invested in a relationship, leaving is extremely difficult.

The one exception to this is an abusive relationship. If there is a physical threat against you or your children, then leaving the marriage, at least until the risk abates, is the reasonable course of action. Research done on women in abusive relationships has found that the big reasons for staying are the investment in the children and the house, as well as the lack of alternatives.[7] That is why shelters for abused women are so important. They give women an alternative to their current situation that will not force them to give up their kids.

Alternatives. The final element of the decision to stay in a relationship is relationship alternatives. Alternatives are simply the options available to you. Is there someone else out there who you want to date? Do you want to be unattached? When a person has many alternatives to her current relationship, she will be less likely to stay in the relationship.

The existence of good alternatives can make people leave satisfying relationships. For example, if you are dating a great guy, but you find out that an even better guy is interested in you, you may leave your romantic relationship. In contrast, a lack of alternatives can make people stay in unsatisfying relationships. For example, if you are dating a relatively rotten guy, but there are no other men out there, you are likely to stay in that bad relationship.

There is another important point to make. Our decisions are driven by our *perception* of reality, not actual reality. For example, a woman may stay in an unsatisfying relationship because she perceives that there are no other good men out there. The truth may be just the opposite. There may be several good men out there, but she may not be aware of them. Remember that nice guys aren't flashy and they take some time to get to know. If you're frequenting the hot spots, you're likely to keep meting and dating narcissists.

There are several factors that may lead to a woman not seeing other decent men out there who she could date. Women with low self-esteem, or who think that they are unattractive, may not realize that there are plenty of other men out there. Women who isolate themselves when they are in a relationship may not notice available men. Also, women who, as a result of a bad relationship history, constantly expect romantic rejection will not notice available men. Sometimes, narcissistic partners will even put their partners down so that they won't leave: "You know, you're lucky to have me; nobody else out there would put up with you."

If you are currently involved with a narcissist, it is important to know if you are only staying in the relationship because you do not believe that you have any alternatives out there. If this were the case, it would be wise to take a second look at your alternatives. Do you have an unrealistically negative opinion of your attractiveness? Do you avoid going out or socializing? Is not dating really so bad? Are you living in Antarctica? It may turn out that you actually have more alternatives than you think. This does not mean that you have to leave the relationship. However, your decision to stay should be based on the actual situation, not a distorted view of the situation.

Should you stay or should you go? To answer this question, it is best to make a careful appraisal of your relationship. Are you satisfied? Is your satisfaction based on the rewards that you receive in the relationship or simply the fact that you have grown to expect lousy treatment from men? How much have you invested in the relationship? Are you simply "throwing good time after bad" by sticking with a loser? Finally, what are your alternatives to the relationships? Are you staying in a bad relationship because you think that you have no alternatives? Is this perception accurate or the result of a poor self-image? Can you make an effort to meet more available men, thereby increasing your alternatives? If you work through these questions and want to stay, then stay. If you work through these questions and want to go, then go.

Chapter Five

Why Do I Always Date Narcissists?

We now know several things about narcissists. We know that they are selfish and manipulative. We know that they make lousy dating partners. We know that they can con women into dating them. We also know that most of the women who do date narcissists eventually realize that it was a real mistake—one that they vow never to repeat.

Regrettably, even with the best intentions, our plans go astray. Some women keep finding themselves in relationships with narcissistic men. We conducted a study (described earlier) where we asked women to describe their relationships with narcissistic men and non-narcissistic men. One of the most enlightening parts of this study, from my perspective, was seeing the comments written by the participants on the research packet. One woman, for example, wrote a note—to us or to herself, I am not certain—under the description of the non-narcissistic man: "Are there really guys like this out there?" Another woman wrote a similar note under the description of the narcissistic man: "Why do I keep dating guys like this?"

These two women seemed to capture a prevalent experience: the feeling that one is swimming in a sea of narcissistic men and that there is no way to avoid getting involved with them. In this section I want to discuss some of the reasons that certain women keep dating narcissistic men. I have touched on several of these ideas in earlier chapters, but I think it is important to explore them thoroughly.

Is It Society's Fault?

The first issue I want to address is the role of society in creating and promoting narcissistic men. Is it society's fault that there are so many narcissistic men? This idea is not as farfetched as it might seem. There are several factors in society that do promote inflated self-opinions and irresponsible dating behavior on the part of men. Taken together, these factors may create the perfect habitat for narcissistic men.

One issue that has been known for a long time by social scientists (but that I have never heard discussed in the media) is the importance of the ratio of males to females in a social group. This sounds complicated, but it is really quite simple. When there are many men and few women in a group, men act in ways that women want them to act. In a sense, women are a limited resource and thus have relationship power. In order to win women's affection, men must offer commitment, affection, and romance. If one man acts like a self-centered jerk, a woman will simply move on to a different man who treats her well. In contrast, when there are many women and few men in a social group, the men become the limited resource and have relationship power. Women will put up with a lot in order to be with a man. If she does not, the man will simply move on to another woman. Guys who are narcissistic jerks will thrive in this environment.

There are several examples in society today where the male-female ratios tilt in the favor of men. That is, there are few men and many women. Surprisingly, one of these is the university. Many universities have dramatically more women than men. To give two examples from my own background, the University of North Carolina has almost a 40/60 male/female ratio. The University of Georgia has a similar ratio. The reason is quite simple. To quote Harry Bellefonte, "the women are smarter." Women are more successful academically than are men and when universities use gender-blind enrollment, they will admit more women than men.

Thus, it is not surprising that narcissistic men thrive on university campuses. They can get away with it because even though some women will figure out their game, there will always be other women out there who are very interested in starting a relationship. I imagine that the narcissistic behavior that men learn they can get away with at big universities carries into their early professional life in big cities like New York, Los Angeles, San Francisco, or Chicago.

The exception to this rule may be engineering and science oriented universities. At technically oriented schools, the ratios get reversed, and you have lots of men but relatively few women. To give another Georgia example, the gender ratio at Georgia Tech is the mirror image of that at the University of Georgia. Georgia Tech has about 30 percent women. In this setting, the women hold much of the social power. According to my students, the women at Georgia Tech have a reputation for being aloof and demanding in their dating life. This makes sense given the gender ratios.

Another social setting where you see a large imbalance between females and males is the inner city. Men are often removed from the population either by early death or by being imprisoned. Like some university campuses, men in these settings can get away with shoddy treatment of women. The current state of rap videos is a testament to this. If the ratios were reversed, men would go back to singing love songs and professing commitment. The problem, of course, is in a social setting where men do not have to commit, family structure breaks down and crime rates rise. This leads to more young men imprisoned, an even bigger male/female discrepancy, even worse treatment of women, and on and on and on....

Strangely, a final setting where these male/female ratios are out of sync is in retirement communities. Men die before women in our society. This is the result of many factors including elevated smoking rates, stress, and lack of attention to health (many men will ignore a health problem rather than go to a doctor).

What has happened in these "sunset communities" is that retired men have started acting like college fraternity members. They date multiple women, they are unfaithful, and they refuse to commit. They can get away with it because there are so few men around and the women are desperate for male attention. The Sun City retirement community is so well known for the flagrant sexual escapades of its members that it has been nicknamed "Sin City!"

Narcissistic men clearly thrive in situations where there are few men and many women. In these settings, women will be much more likely to tolerate men's game playing and infidelity.

Another societal factor that promotes narcissism is one that I had described in the section "Changing Places, Changing Faces." Once all the women in a social group have learned who the narcissists are, the ability of the narcissists to manipulate women is diminished. This should happen relatively quickly in a stable social environment, for example, a small town where everyone knows each other and few people move in or out. In the small town, women will be able to quickly single out and avoid narcissistic men.

In social environments where there is a constant turnover of individuals, narcissists will be much more able to keep their true character hidden. Women who are new to these constantly changing social settings will be immediately approached by the resident narcissists. Sure, the new women will wise up after a while, but at that point, the narcissists will move to new victims.

There are several settings that fit this description. Universities are one such place. Roughly one fourth of the student body changes every year. After four years, there is an entirely new student body on campus. Narcissists will thrive in these situations. There will always be naïve women entering campus—and they will not be able to identify the narcissists. Big cities are another example: Los Angeles, New York, Atlanta, and Chicago. Every year a new batch of job seekers enters these environments. They do not know anyone, and the narcissists are there to date them. Narcissists can get away with their selfish behavior because there is a constant supply of new women. There is a reason that dramas like *Sex and the City* take place in New York and not Des Moines.

Where there is stability, people will know each other's character and behaviors. Narcissists will be found out relatively quickly. Where there is a constant inflow and outflow of people, the narcissists will not be as easily identified. They will thrive.

Finally, we must ask ourselves if there are other trends in society that promote narcissistic behavior. Does society do things that encourage narcissistic behavior among its boys and young men? I believe that the answer is "yes." In particular, the increased focus of society on self-esteem and self-gratification may promote narcissistic behavior. This starts with the "self-esteem movement" in schools. Children are taught to love themselves. They are sheltered from failing and punishment because that might "damage their self-esteem." Teachers and parents are highly concerned with sheltering students from the negative consequences of their behavior. Instead, they want them to be happy and popular.

From my perspective, the self-esteem movement is absurd—especially for boys. Young adults in our society have extremely high self-esteem—and it has been getting higher and higher since we started measuring it. At the same time, there have been no demonstrable benefits from this increased emphasis on self-esteem. Instead, there has, at least anecdotally, been an increase in spoiled, entitled children. Clearly, many kids will grow out of this when they get jobs and families and are forced to take responsibility for their lives. Unfortunately, it would be reasonable to expect more narcissistic men far into the future.[1]

Let me reiterate that even in the worst of settings, not all men will be narcissistic. Instead, men who have a tendency to be narcissistic in their relationships will be better able to get away with their antics in certain social environments. Where there are few men and many women, where there is a constant inflow of new people, and where young men are taught to develop self-esteem rather than character, you will find a large number of narcissistic men.

Is It The Narcissist's Fault?

Society almost certainly contributes to the rash of narcissism in this country. In different circumstances, we would have fewer narcissists—or at least the narcissists out there would be more easily identified and avoided. Does that mean that the narcissists themselves are *not* responsible for their own actions? Are they victims of society, bad parenting, or cosmic forces? For several reasons, I think that the answer to all these questions is "no." I think narcissists should be held accountable for their own actions.

First, and I cannot stress this enough, narcissists *like* being narcissists. They *want* to be narcissists. Narcissists do not stay up at night thinking, "Why do I feel so good about myself? Why am I such a good-looking guy? Why am I so much better than everyone else? I must change!" Narcissists look at the mirror and think, "I rock!"

To the best of my knowledge, narcissists do not suffer psychologically from their condition. Instead, everyone around them suffers. This idea is very hard to swallow. It suggests, "narcissism pays." Unfortunately, I think that this statement is true in many ways. Narcissists are happy, extroverted, and confident. They have high self-esteem and love looking at themselves in the mirror. They think that they are special and unique individuals. In each narcissist's little fantasy world, he is king.

Many researchers and clinicians seem unable to accept this proposition. I even include myself in this camp sometimes. We find it very difficult to accept that narcissists "get away with" being such arrogant jerks. It affronts our sense of justice. Frankly, it stinks to spend your life trying to be a decent and compassionate person only to watch narcissists strut around with the glow of success.

Many of us have tried to find those areas in which narcissists do suffer. Some psychologists think that deep inside narcissists have a hidden vulnerability. They are truly lonely children who crave affection. Their narcissism is just a sham or an act that allows them to protect their vulnerable inner core. Other psychologists think that narcissists might feel good when they are young, but that they will suffer in old age when their hair falls out and no one wants to go to their parties anymore. Freud thought that narcissists would eventually grow sick because they were missing real connection with others. I tend to think that if narcissists spend their lives gloating on their own success and "specialness," they must be missing the deep satisfaction that comes with connecting to the world. As I type this, I am drinking a great cup of dark Sumatran coffee and watching two cardinals in the trees outside my office window. This is much more rewarding to me than thinking about how special I am—but what do I know? I would probably be much happier if I thought that I was God's gift to the world.

Although narcissists do seem to feel good, there is some evidence that narcissists' relentless pursuit of status and esteem makes them do stupid things. For example, narcissists' are chronically overconfident in their abilities. Occasionally, this leads to problems. For example, when narcissists bet, they are more likely than others to lose money. In addition, some studies have found that narcissists do poorly at universities—even though they think they will do better than everyone else. Narcissists can shoot themselves in the foot by letting their own arrogance and entitlement get the best of them. President Clinton, for example, lost the potential to make some major changes to the country because he was so busy trying to cover up an affair with an intern.[2]

In all, narcissists seem to do reasonably well in modern society. They reap some psychological benefits and suffer some decision-making consequences. We all hope that they will someday get their "just rewards" psychologically speaking, but I do not know if this will be the case.

Second, I think that although narcissism is, in part, a result of genetics and parenting, narcissists make little effort to change. Society does not force narcissists to act like narcissistic jerks against their will. Rather, I believe that society allows people who have narcissistic tendencies to bloom into full-fledged narcissists. Our society is often fertile soil for the seeds of narcissism. You might think that because narcissists did not choose to be narcissists at age eighteen, but rather were born and raised with some tendency to be narcissistic, they are not really responsible for their behavior. I would disagree with that conclusion.

To start with, many people are born and raised with certain personality characteristics that can cause others to suffer. In most cases, these people suffer themselves and struggle to change. For example, depressed people are often no fun to be around. They can bring others down. Still, we feel for people with depression because they are suffering and because they are trying to change. Likewise, people with obsessive traits can be tough to be around. They might spend too much time double and triple checking the locks and appear nervous. However, they too suffer and often try to change. Thus, we sympathize with them. Narcissists, however, are different. They hurt others, but rarely make any effort to change. Thus, they are partly responsible for their situation.

You might counter with, "But you said narcissism was very difficult to change, so how can we expect narcissists to change their behavior? I still feel sorry for them and I wish that I could help narcissistic men." I think that this is the wrong way to go. Narcissists typically do not even *try* to change their behavior. They may, on occasion, go into therapy, but will often leave as soon as they get some positive feedback from the therapist. They do not enter therapy to change their narcissistic ways; they just want to get back to feeling good about themselves. The only exception that I have noticed is that some people who are mildly narcissistic will realize that sometimes their narcissism gets the better of them. This is especially likely to happen in social settings like parties. They will try to control this obvious narcissism because it turns people off.

Additionally, narcissists could remain narcissists, but try to act in a way that benefited rather than detracted from others. I remember a story that I read about Donald Trump years ago. He wanted to display his own prowess as a builder/developer and let New York know how much better he was than the city government at getting the job done. To do this, he built the ice-rink in Central Park in record time. Sure, this was in part a narcissistic act, but it helped improve the quality of life for a lot of people. Bottom line: Narcissists can try to direct their narcissistic strivings to positive ends. This is great, and I respect people who do this, but most do not.

Finally, narcissists not only like being narcissists and do not try to change their personality, but they also just do not care too much about other people. Thinking about this brings to mind the old story of the scorpion and the frog.

The frog and the scorpion were standing by the shore of a pond. The scorpion approached the frog and said, "Please give me a ride across the pond on your back."

The frog replied, "But if I give you a ride, you will sting me and I will drown."

The scorpion countered, "If I sting you, we both will drown, so I will certainly not sting you."

The frog thought that this made sense. Why would the scorpion sting him if it would mean the scorpion's own death? So the frog decided to carry the scorpion across the pond. Halfway to the other side the scorpion stung the frog. As he started sinking, the frog said, "Why did you sting me? Now we both will drown."

The scorpion replied, "Because it is my nature."

I sometimes think that narcissists are the same way. Imagine a narcissist who gets in a relationship with a woman who really cares about him. Like the frog, she might think, "Everything is great, so why would he hurt me?" But the narcissist does because it is his nature to do so. He does not care about other people as much as he cares about himself. In general, narcissists are not blind to the effect of their actions on others.

To return to the question raised at the beginning of this section, I think that narcissists are largely responsible for their own behaviors. Yes, they have some basic predisposition and early experiences that send them in the direction of becoming narcissists, and, yes, society certainly makes it easy for narcissists to flourish, but narcissists are far from blameless. Narcissists like being narcissists and they do not want to change. Narcissists also do not care about other people's feelings. Keep in mind that they are not incapable of gauging other's feelings. Quite to the contrary, they need to be able to "read" others' feelings in order to manipulate them. Narcissists just do not care about others. In short, it is narcissists' fault that they are narcissistic jerks.

Remember that narcissists can be amazingly manipulative. After abusing you again and again, they may still want to keep a relationship going. Maybe they want your admiration, money, or who knows what. They might try a play for your sympathy. *I know I can be a bad guy, but it is not my fault. My dad was cold and uncaring and my mom spoiled me. You are the only one who sees the real me. Please let me stay, I will try to change. I love you.* DO NOT FALL FOR THIS. I have heard this story too many times. It is not that difficult to treat people with respect. If narcissists do not do it, it is because they do not *want* to do it. If you really want to have a relationship with the person, have him get his act together and then come back. Do not let him stay around on the pretext that he will change. Think about it. If you want to teach a dog to shake hands, you do not give him a biscuit and then wait for him to shake. Instead, you wait for him to shake and then give him a biscuit. The same holds for narcissists.

Is It My Fault?

Why do you keep dating narcissists? First, our society keeps making narcissists. Today, there are several rewards for narcissists and the forces that traditionally held narcissists in check are not as prevalent. Second, the narcissists who are made do not want to change. Narcissists like being narcissists and do not have a great deal of concern about hurting others. The question addressed in this section is whether the narcissists' victims are to blame for their relationships. If you repeatedly date narcissistic men, is it your fault?

Everyone has painful relationships from time to time. Contrary to popular opinion, practically no one intentionally seeks out suffering. There is no hidden, unconscious, or secret aspect of a person that says "I want to be miserable" or "I want keep getting hurt in relationships." People do make bad choices. They might date exciting guys who eventually hurt them. This is not because they want to get hurt. It is because they like exciting guys. If the guys had a big "N" on their shirts for "narcissist" and told the women that they would hurt them, the decision would be different. "Hey, let's have a short-term, exciting relationship, and when you want more intimacy, I will lie to you, get drunk and hit on your friends, and blame you for not being a good enough girlfriend. How does that sound?" Unfortunately, narcissists are more clever than that.

The same can be said for dieting. No one wants to be obese. Some people enjoy rich food; they do not like the long-term outcome of eating rich food. Narcissistic men are more difficult to avoid than cake—chocolate cake does not hit on you at a bar or disguise itself as spinach salad.

The bottom line is that it makes little sense to say, "It is my fault that I always date narcissistic men." No one repeatedly sets out to get hurt.

That said, it is likely that there are one or more factors that influence your repeated dating of narcissistic men. The key is to identify these factors and try to change them. This involves taking *responsibility* for your situation rather than blaming yourself for your situation. These seem like the same thing, but they are very different.

When you say it is my *fault* that I keep dating narcissistic men, that implies that there is some stable part of yourself that wants the current state of affairs to continue. You might think that it is an unconscious leftover from your childhood, a reflection of your inability to function in the social world, or simply your destiny. Fault implies that there is a crack in your being that dictates bad things happening.

Believing that one is at fault for dating narcissists leads to several negative outcomes. First, you think that there is little you can do to change. There is something deeply wrong with you, and beyond seven years of psychotherapy, there is little that you can do about it. Second, you get depressed or dejected because you know that nothing will change and because you think that there is something wrong with you. Third, you do things to make yourself feel less depressed. This is fine if you do something healthy like running or yoga. Unfortunately, most people who are depressed go with the real short-term fixes. The most popular are binge eating and drinking alcohol. Women tend to go for the food and guys tend to go for the booze. Both make you fat and leave you even more dejected. Fourth, you think, "What the hell, this is my destiny to date narcissistic men, so I might as well enjoy it and give up trying to find anything better." This sounds good in theory, but does little to improve your situation.

The alternative to blaming yourself for your situation is taking *responsibility* for your situation. Responsibility implies that (a) the situation that you are in does *not* reflect some global aspect of your personality (e.g., you are not a bad person or cursed), and (b) that you can effectively change your circumstance. Responsibility entails saying something like: "I am not the bad person here." There is nothing wrong with me, but there are steps I can take to improve my own situation. If I don't do it, who will?

Taking responsibility for your situation has several positive outcomes. You do not view yourself as a "bad" person. To the contrary, you view yourself as someone who has the power to change her environment. Your situation becomes a challenge rather than a failure. The possibility for change is given. Psychologically, this changes you. Instead of getting depressed and dejected, you become energized and excited. Confronting a challenge brings out the best in people. When you feel good, you make positive changes in your life. This leads to a greater perception of control, which leads to even more positive changes. The result is a sense of personal power and efficacy. As my uncle always used to say to me when I bungled various personal issues, *responsibility is the ability to respond.* This is a good thing.

So, you do the smart thing and do not blame yourself for your situation. Instead, you realize that your relationships with narcissistic men are not your fault, but you want to take responsibility for changing them. How do you effectively take responsibility for your situation? I address this in the next section.

Never Dating a Narcissist Again

If you are one of those people who finds herself in relationships with one narcissist after another—and I hear that story a lot—your biggest question probably is: How can I stop dating narcissistic men? There are four basic strategies to keep narcissists out of your relationship life: Understanding narcissism, understanding your attraction process, looking at the situations where you meet men, and cutting your losses.

Understanding narcissism. This is a problem that I have heard from many women. They have dated really lousy men, but have no idea what it was exactly about these men that was the problem. They knew they were self-centered, not very caring, vain, and, perhaps, unfaithful, but they didn't put all these pieces together. It never clicked that this guy was just a narcissist, because they did not know what narcissism was all about.

The reason that it is important to understand narcissism is that it makes excuse-making more difficult. If you think that your boyfriend is a pretty good guy, except for a few unrelated problems like some overcontrolling behavior, potential infidelity, vanity, and materialism, you are likely to make excuses for each of these behaviors. Sure, he can be overcontrolling, but that is his way of dealing with the stresses of life, and sure, he can be vain, but at least he isn't a slob like some guys. By understanding narcissism, you will see that these behaviors are part of a larger pattern. You will also notice other behaviors that seemed odd, but didn't seem to fit in with any larger pattern. Almost invariably when I talk to women about narcissism, they think of some past relationship and say things like: "Oh yeah, that explains the way he always switched the topic to himself when we talked," or "Oh yeah, I always wondered why he would want to check my outfits before we went out." Hopefully, if you have read the book this far, you have a much better ability than you did before to identify narcissistic patterns in men.

Understanding your attraction process. What is it about you that is drawn to narcissistic men? One of the best ways to avoid dating narcissists is to stop the dating process at the stage of initial attraction. As we have discussed, there are certain characteristics that make narcissists attractive: Extroversion, confidence, and charm, for example. There is also the feeling of excitement and immediate attraction that seems to arise in relationships with narcissists. With nice guys, the relationships usually move more slowly, with more emotional intimacy and friendship.

I have had several women tell me that they like certain traits that narcissistic men seem to possess in spades. They like men who are confident, ambitious, energetic, and highly social. They also do not like men who are—and I have heard this phrase many times—"too nice." Yes, there are many men who have this combination of traits and who are not narcissists. At the same time, most narcissistic men also have these traits. So, if you are searching for an ambitious and exciting man who is not "too nice," you are likely to be drawn to many narcissists. Also, if you are always looking for excitement rather than emotional closeness you are more likely to be drawn to narcissists.

In what I consider to be a slightly more extreme situation, women also can use relationships to meet their own narcissistic needs. They are attracted to men who show them off in public, dramatize the relationship, and make them feel sophisticated or important. Unfortunately, narcissistic men are often more than happy to fulfill these needs. Nice guys are more interested in fun and companionship.

So, what do you do? First, slow it down. Take your time to form a friendship with someone before you start dating. Narcissists' charms tend to diminish, so with time the real person will become clear.

Second, the heart and the gut are good, but so is the brain. Attraction isn't all about chemistry—so base your decisions on more than chemistry. Someone once told me that after a string of bad relationships, she decided that anytime she was at a party and felt undeniably drawn to a man, she would run. She didn't know what the problem was exactly, but he knew that the "chemistry" she felt in the attraction process was leading to some poor choices. Instead, she tried to spend time with people where the chemistry wasn't as strong, but the affection and friendship were stronger.

Third, do what a scientist would do and collect data on a person before becoming involved. What is his dating history? What do your friends think? Who are his friends? Do the stories that he tells you make sense? I am not suggesting an FBI background check or private investigator, but a reasonable effort to check someone out makes sense. I talked to a reporter about some of these ideas, and she said, "Oh yeah, you need to get a resumé on a prospective partner." Her point was that the best way to see how someone will be with you is to see how they were with other people. I should also note that you don't rely on a narcissist's view of his relationship past. "I had eight bad relationships, but it was always the women's fault." Chances are, you are only getting one side of the story.

Finally, whatever you do, do not talk yourself into a relationship with a narcissist. If all these bells are going off in your head saying that this is a bad guy, and your friends think the same things, and his history is suspect, do not start making excuses because of chemistry. You might tell yourself that your friends are jealous, or that all his ex-girlfriends are psychos who spread unfair rumors, but this is a mistake.

Look at the situation where you meet people. A final question to ask is: What is it about my situation that leads me to meet narcissistic men? The problem may have less to do with your ability to pick out narcissists than your social situation. It could be that you keep putting yourself in situations where narcissists tend to congregate.

As social psychologists have known for decades, one of the biggest predictors of who you will end up dating is who you spend time with. If you spend time with narcissists, you will end up dating narcissists. So become aware of where you socialize. Are you hanging out with narcissistic men—bars? the dating scene in most big cities? fraternity parties or their adult equivalent? If so, you will end up dating narcissists.

The way to avoid this is to start meeting men in different situations. You might join a club or some other organization that you are interested in and meet men there. These could be anything from outdoor groups to church or synagogue organizations. If you are doing something that you enjoy, and which helps you grow as a person, you will be getting a benefit. Meeting someone will be a bonus. You can also have your friends introduce you to potential partners. This doesn't always work, of course, but it is usually better than meeting men at bars. The truth is that you now want to meet a decent guy, and your goal is to change the odds in your favors by minimizing the number of narcissists that you come in contact with.

Cutting your losses. Even if you make all the efforts described above, you can still end up with a narcissist. The key at this point is to cut your losses and move on. As we discussed earlier, it gets harder and harder to leave a relationship the more that you have invested in it. The more time that you put into it, the more that you want things to work out. This may be especially true if you are coming off a string of bad relationships—you may get desperate for one to work out. This is understandable emotionally, but doesn't make sense rationally. The smart thing to do if you find yourself going down the same relationship path with a narcissistic man is to get out and try again. It is always tough to leave a relationship—but it only gets tougher as the relationship progresses. Furthermore, as long as you are in a relationship with a jerk, you are missing opportunities to meet a decent guy.

Here is a set of concrete steps that you might want to think about for avoiding narcissistic men.

1. Look for narcissistic behavior patterns. If a guy spends lots of time in front of the mirror, talks incessantly about material possession, and flirts with your cousin, you may have a problem.
2. Do not focus on initial looks: Sure, looks matter in a boyfriend, but remember that your judgments of someone's looks change as you get to know them. Nice guys become more attractive; narcissists become less attractive.
3. Do not mistake "chemical" attraction for love: Your chemistry can give you all sorts of "go" signals when you meet a man. This is not the same as love.
4. Go slow: Relationships that last a long time can take a long time to start. Do not think that if you are not in love after 15 minutes you never will be.
5. Focus on friendship: Narcissists are less likely to want close, warm friendships. Change your strategy for meeting men: e.g., date "friends of friends," not men who approach you at bars.

6. Do not talk yourself into a relationship with a narcissist: If you start dating someone—and all the signals are that he is a narcissist—leave. There are plenty of decent men out there.

7. Listen to your friends: When narcissists are working their magic on a woman, it is often difficult for her to see him for what he is. The good news is that her friends often can.

8. Avoid a man who acts like a narcissist to others: I have heard women say that they know a man loves them because he is arrogant and mean to everyone else, but nice to them. It won't last.

9. Avoid a man with a bad reputation. Narcissists do not often change. If a man has been a narcissist in the past, he probably still is one.

10. If you know that the person that you are forming a dating relationship with is a narcissist, cut your losses and leave. The longer you stay, the harder it will be to leave.

In sum, dating a series of narcissists does not mean that you are bad or cursed or self-destructive. It is in your best interest, however, to take responsibility for your situation. The simple act of taking control will itself increase your sense of well-being. Understand why you date narcissistic men. Once that question is answered, the desired life changes can be made more effectively.

If you think the problem is your discrimination in selecting men, work on understanding better the men that you are attracted to before you date them. Find out about their past relationships. Get your friends' opinions of them. See how they act in a variety of situations and to people that they are not trying to manipulate. If they seem okay at this point, you may want to wade in a bit, but maintain your awareness. If you think that the problem is your social environment you should change your environment. This is usually tough psychologically because we get comfortable with the way that we live. If you have dated three narcissistic men in the past and met them at bars, try to avoid meeting men at bars. If you meet narcissistic men at your office, then stop dating guys at work. You may then want to try some other social setting to meet men: group activities like a softball league, church/synagogue, etc.

When you make these changes, remember to do a couple of things. First, give it some time. Change is difficult so do not expect it to take place right away. Second, keep records of what you are doing. Who are you meeting? What are you thinking about the people that you meet? Where are you meeting people? What is the outcome? One suggestion would be to keep a journal of your social interactions. By keeping records, you will over time develop a deeper awareness of the choices that you make and why you make them. This in turn can be used to direct successful changes in the future. Finally, have faith that change will come. Many women who chronically were attracted to narcissistic men have changed. Borrowing a term from one of these women, they "flipped the switch."

Flipping the switch. Many women have throughout their lives consistently dated narcissistic men. They had a string of bad relationships, but did not immediately identify their selection of men as the problem. These men tended to be successful, popular, and ambitious. From an outsider's perspective, these may have been great relationships. Inside the relationships, however, there were always the classic problems associated with dating narcissists, such as lack of emotional intimacy, competitiveness, and infidelity. Still, these relationships "felt right." It seemed natural to be involved with someone self-centered and assertive. Guys that weren't like that just seemed a bit too wimpy.

After a string of these relationships, however, most of these women began to get an inkling that there was a problem. At first they thought it was them, maybe they were not warm enough or they expected too much. Then they thought the problem might have to do with the situation. The lack of emotional intimacy might be caused by their professional lives interfering with their relationships. Finally, however, they came to the conclusion that they were getting involved with the wrong type of man, and repeating this pattern over and over.

Of course, it is one thing to know in your head that you are making a mistake, but it is another thing to know in your heart. Even after these women eventually realized that the men that they kept getting involved with were the problem, they still felt attracted to narcissistic men. They kept mistaking arrogance and coldness for strength—and they didn't really want to be with a weak man.

So, they wrestled with this issue for months or even years, trying to reconcile their hearts and heads. Then, each of these women described having a similar experience. It became clear to her at a very fundamental level that she was attracted to the wrong guy. These revelations have been described to me as "a switch flipping on" or "a light bulb going on in my head." Sometimes the flipping of the switch was dramatic; sometimes it seemed to happen over the course of a few weeks or a month. Regardless, after the switch was flipped these women were no longer attracted to narcissistic men. Narcissists had simply lost their appeal. Instead, they were attracted to men that cared deeply about them.

This switch flipping process seems to be the result of the mental awareness of narcissistic relationships making its way from the head to the heart. I have heard this same story from enough different women that I believe it is a real and important experience. Also, what is appealing about this is that it means that there is not a lifetime of resisting narcissistic men. Rather, at some point this desire just goes away. Imagine constantly craving chocolate, and then trying to go on a diet. It is very difficult to eat asparagus when what feels right to you is chocolate; however, if something inside of you clicks and the chocolate cravings simply vanish, it becomes much easier to have a healthy diet. The same experience can occur in relationships, with the healthy partner becoming the natural choice.

Conclusions. This week, I gave the narcissism lecture in my romantic relationships class that I give every semester. Like every time I give the lecture, I heard the classic stories of various ex-boyfriends: The guy who said (while referring to himself, not an actual car), "Why drive a Pinto when you can drive a Mercedes."

The boyfriend who broke up with his girlfriend every holiday because he thought that he might meet someone better on vacation. The evil Eddie Haskell boyfriend who was adored by the parents but rotten in the relationship. The boyfriend who was entering the film industry and said, "I just can't be seen with you anymore. You would be bad for my image." The med school boyfriend who ordered Crown Royal at bars and smoked expensive cigars even though he was $100,000 in debt. It is clear that narcissists continue making a mess of people's romantic lives. My hope is that by reading this book you will be able to avoid this mess in the future.

Research Notes (By Section)

Most of the ideas in this book are derived from and verified by academic research. Other ideas are derived from work in the areas of clinical psychology and psychiatry. Several of these ideas are informed speculation on my part. In order to clarify which is which I have included this listing of research articles and relevant readings. I have organized this list by section. I hope that this list is a good starting point for those interested in learning about narcissism in more depth.

Chapter 1: Who is a Narcissist?
What is Narcissism?

[1]Campbell, W. K., Reeder, G. D., Sedikides, C., & Elliot, A. J. (2000). Narcissism and comparative self-enhancement strategies. *Journal of Research in Personality,* 34, 329-347.

[2]The NPI was first presented in:

Raskin, R. & Hall, C. S. (1979) A narcissistic personality inventory. *Psychological Reports,* 45, 590.

Two others papers present short forms of the measure as well as some validation information:

Emmons, R. A. (1984). Factor analysis and construct validity of the narcissistic personality inventory. *Journal of Personality Assessment,* 48, 291–300.

Raskin, R. N., & Terry, H. (1988). A principle components analysis of the Narcissistic Personality Inventory and further evidence of its construct validity. *Journal of Personality and Social Psychology,* 54, 890–902

Damn, I'm Good (but I'm No Mother Teresa)

[3]Robins, R. W., & John, O. P. (1997). Effects of visual perspective and narcissism on self-perception: Is seeing believing? *Psychological Science,* 8, 37–42.

[4]Kernis, M. H. (2003) Toward a conceptualization of optimal self-esteem. *Psychological Inquiry,* 14, 1–26.

[5]Rosenberg, M. (1965). *Society and the adolescent self-image.* Princeton, NJ: Princeton University Press.

[6]Wallace, H. M., & Baumeister, R. F. (2002). The performance of narcissists rises and falls with perceived opportunity for glory. *Journal of Personality and Social Psychology,* 82, 819–834.

[7]Campbell, W. K., Rudich, E., & Sedikides, C. (2002). Narcissism, self-esteem, and the positivity of self-views: Two portraits of self-love. *Personality and Social Psychology Bulletin,* 28, 358–368.

[8]Gabriel, M. T., Critelli, J. W., & Ee, J. S. (1994). Narcissistic illusions in self-evaluations of intelligence and attractiveness. *Journal of Personality, 62,* 143–155.

Entitlement—Narcissist's Secret Ingredient

[9]Campbell, W. K., Bonacci, A. M., Shelton, J., Exline, J. J., & Bushman, B. J. (2004). Psychological entitlement: Interpersonal consequences and validation of a new self-report measure. *Journal of Personality Assessment, 83,* 29–45.

Mr. Fun

[10]Baumeister, R. F., & Vohs, K. D. (2001). Narcissism as addiction to esteem. *Psychological Inquiry, 12,* 206-210.

[11]Hogan, R., & Hogan, J. (2002). Assessing leadership: A view from the dark side. *International Journal of Selection and Assessment, 9,* 40–51.

Do Not Look at the Man Behind the Curtain (or, Maintaining The Narcissist's Illusion)

[12]Buss, D. M., & Chiodo, L. M. (1991). Narcissistic acts in everyday life. *Journal of Personality, 59,* 179–215.

[13]Raskin, R. N., & Novacek, J. (1991). Narcissism and the use of fantasy. *Journal of Clinical Psychology, 47,* 490–499.

[14]Raskin, R. N., & Shaw, R. (1988). Narcissism and the use of personal pronouns. *Journal of Personality, 56,* 393–404.

When the Bubble Bursts (or, What Happens When The Truth Breaks Through)

[15]Bushman, B. J., & Baumeister, R. F. (1998). Threatened egotism, narcissism, self-esteem, and direct and displaced aggression: Does self-love or self-hate lead to violence? *Journal of Personality and Social Psychology, 75,* 219–229.

[16]Twenge, J., & Campbell, W. K. (2003). "Isn't it fun to get the respect that we're going to deserve?" Narcissism, social rejection, and aggression. *Personality and Social Psychology Bulletin, 29,* 261–272.

Six Other Questions about Narcissists

[17]Horton, R. S., Bleau G., & Drwecki, B. (2004). Parenting narcissus: Does parenting contribute to the development of narcissism? *Manuscript under review.*

[18]I discuss this view in more detail in: Campbell, W. K. (2001). Is narcissism really so bad? *Psychological Inquiry, 12,* 214–216.

[19]There is still much disagreement in the field about the "deep down inside" model of narcissism. For a contrasting view, see Jordan, C. H., Spencer, S. J., Zanna, M. P., Hoshino-Browne, E., & Correll, J. (2003). Secure and defensive high self-esteem. *Journal of Personality and Social Psychology, 85,* 969–978. My opinion is that their findings are confounded by their communal measure of implicit self-esteem. Furthermore, even with this measure, they did not find low implicit self-esteem on the part of narcissists. Nevertheless, I do not have the data to offer more than an opinion and additional research could come out on either side of this debate.

[20]Millon, T., Millon, C., Davis, R. (1994). *Millon Clinical Multi-axial Inventory-III (MCMI-III) Manual.* Minneapolis: National Computer Systems.

[21]Foster, J. D., Campbell, W. K., & Twenge, J. M. (2003). Individual differences in narcissism: Inflated self-views across the lifespan and around the world. *Journal of Research in Personality, 37,* 469–486.

[22]Dabbs, J. M., Jr., with Dabbs, M. G. (2000). Heroes, Rogues & Lovers: Testosterone and Behavior. New York: McGraw-Hill.

Chapter 2: Narcissists in Relationships
Being the Top Dog (or, It's All About Winning)

[1]Baumeister, R. F., & Bratslavsky, E. (1999). Passion, intimacy, and time: Passionate love as a function of change in intimacy. *Personality and Social Psychology Review, 3,* 49–67.

[2]Campbell, W. K. (1999). Narcissism and romantic attraction. *Journal of Personality and Social Psychology, 77,* 1254–1270.

[3]Brunell, A. B., Campbell, W. K., Smith, L., & Krusemark, E. A. (2004, February). *Why do people date narcissists? A narrative study.* Poster presented at the annual meeting of the Society for Personality and Social Psychology, Austin, TX.

[4]Alicke, M. D. (1985). Global self-evaluations as determined by the desirability and controllability of trait adjectives. *Journal of Personality and Social Psychology, 49,* 1621–1630.

[5]Alicke, M. D., Klotz, M. L., Breitenbecher, D. L., Yurak, T. J., & Vredenberg, D. S. (1995). Personal contact, individuation, and the better-than-average effect. *Journal of Personality and Social Psychology, 68,* 804–825.

[6]For a good discussion of these issues in marriage, see: Beach, S. R. H., Tesser, A., Mendolia, M., & Page, A. (1996). Self-evaluation maintenance in marriage: Toward a performance ecology of the marital relationship. *Journal of Family Psychology, 10*, 379–396. A similar study with narcissism is: Morf, C. C., & Rhodewalt, F. (1993). Narcissism and self-evaluation maintenance: Explorations in object relations. *Personality and Social Psychology Bulletin, 19*, 668–676.

[7]Campbell, W. K., Rudich, E., & Sedikides, C. (2002). Narcissism, self-esteem, and the positivity of self-views: Two portraits of self-love. *Personality and Social*
Psychology Bulletin, 28, 358–368.

I'm in Control Here

[8]Baumeister, R. F., Catanese, K. R., & Wallace, H. M. (2002). Conquest by force: A narcissistic reactance theory of rape and sexual coercion. *Review of General Psychology*, 6, 92–135.

Bushman, B. J., Bonacci, A. M., van Dijk, M., & Baumeister, R. F. (2003). Narcissism, sexual refusal, and aggression: Testing a narcissistic reactance model of sexual coercion. *Journal of Personality and Social Psychology*, 84, 1027–1040.

Empathy? Caring? Huh?

Can We Talk About Me for a Moment?

[9]Vangelisti, A., Knapp, M. L., & Daly, J. A. (1990). Conversational narcissism. *Communication Monographs, 57*, 251–274.

[10]Tracy, J. L., & Robins, R. W. (2004). Show your pride: Evidence for a discrete emotion expression. *Psychological Science,* 15, 194–197

Wandering Eyes (or, What You Don't Know Won't Hurt You)

[11]The full scale can be found in: Miller, R. S. (1997). Inattentive and contented: Relationship commitment and attention to alternatives. *Journal of Personality and Social Psychology, 73,* 758–766.

[12]Emmons, R. A. (1991). Relationship between narcissism and sensation seeking. *Journal of Social Behavior and Personality, 6,* 943–954.

[13]Schmitt, D. P., & Buss, D. M. (2001). Human mate poaching: Tactics and temptations for infiltrating existing mateships. *Journal of Personality and Social Psychology,* 80, 894–917.

[14]Foster, J.D., Shrira, I., & Campbell, W. K. (2004, February). *Exploring relationships that results when a partner is attracted away from a previous partner.* Poster presented at the annual meeting of the Society for Personality and Social Psychology, Austin, TX.

[15]Campbell, W. K., Foster, C. A., & Finkel, E. J. (2002). Does self-love lead to love for others? A story of narcissistic game playing. *Journal of Personality and Social Psychology,* 83, 340–354.

Commitment is Great—For Other People (or, "The List")

[16]Rusbult, C. E. (1980). Commitment and satisfaction in romantic associations: A test of the investment model. *Journal of Personality and Social Psychology,* 38, 172–186.

Rusbult, C. E. (1983). A longitudinal test of the investment model: The development (and deterioration) of satisfaction and commitment in heterosexual involvements. *Journal of Personality and Social Psychology,* 45, 101–117.

[17]Campbell, W. K., & Foster, C. A. (2002). Narcissism and commitment in romantic relationships: An Investment Model analysis. *Personality and Social Psychology Bulletin,* 28, 484–495.

[18]Agnew, C. R., Van Lange, P. A. M., Rusbult, C. E., & Langston, C. A. (1998). Cognitive interdependence: Commitment and the mental representation of close relationships. *Journal of Personality and Social Psychology,* 74, 939–954.

[19]Rusbult, C. E., Verette, J., Whitney, G. A., Slovik, L. F., & Lipkus, I. (1991). Accommodation processes and close relationships: Theory and preliminary empirical evidence. *Journal of Personality and Social Psychology,* 60, 53–78.

[20]Gottman, J. (1994). Why marriages succeed or fail. New York: Simon & Schuster.

[21]Foster, J.D., Shrira, I., & Campbell, W. K. (2003, February). *An experimental test of the "Core and Explore" mating strategy.* Poster presented at the annual of the Society for Personality and Social Psychology, Los Angeles, CA.

What do Narcissists Call Love?

[22]Sternberg, R. J. (1986). A triangular theory of love. *Psychological Review*, 93, 119–135.

[23]Hendrick, C, & Hendrick, S. S. (1986). A theory and method of love. *Journal of Personality and Social Psychology,* 50, 392–402.

These lovestyles are typically presented with their Greek names: Erotic = Eros, game playing = ludus, companionate = storge, pragmatic = pragma, lovesick = mania, and selfless = agape.

[24]Most of the ideas in this Chapter are detailed in: Campbell, W. K., Foster, C. A., & Finkel, E. J. (2002). Does self-love lead to love for others? A story of narcissistic game playing. *Journal of Personality and Social Psychology, 83*, 340–354.

Bling, Bling: Narcissism and Materialism

[25]American Psychiatric Association (2000). *Diagnostic and Statistical Manual of Mental Disorders, Fourth Edition, Text Revision (DSM-IV®-TR)*. APA.

[26]Buss, D. M. (1994). *The evolution of desire.* New York: Basic Books.

[27]Clark, R. D. & Hatfield, E. (1989). Gender differences in receptivity to sexual offers. *Journal of Psychology and Human Sexuality, 2*, 39–55.

Manipulative Weasels—Emotion and Deception

[28]The best evidence for this comes from: Campbell, W. K., Foster, C. A., & Finkel, E. J. (2002). Does self-love lead to love for others? A story of narcissistic game playing. *Journal of Personality and Social Psychology, 83*, 340–354. More research needs to be done, however. As it stand, this section involves a reasonable amount of speculation.

Changing Places, Changing Faces

Chapter 3: Why Get Involved with a Narcissist?

Making a Big Entrance

[1]Tice, D. M., Butler, J. L., Muraven, M. B., & Stillwell, A. M. (1995). When modesty prevails: Differential favorability of self-presentation to friends and strangers. *Journal of Personality and Social Psychology*, 69, 1120–1138.

[2]Oltmanns, T. F., Friedman, J. N., Fiedler, E. R., & Turkheimer, E. (2004). Perceptions of people with personality disorders based on thin slices of behavior. *Journal of Research in Personality,* 38, 216–229.

The Old Bait and Switch

[3]Sedikides, C., Oliver, M. B., & Campbell, W. K. (1994). Perceived benefits and costs of romantic relationships for women and men: Implications for exchange theory. *Personal Relationships,* 1, 5–21.

The Illusion That Other People are Like You

[4]Ross, L., Greene, D. & House, P. (1977). The false consensus effect: An egocentric bias in social perception and attributional processes. *Journal of Experimental Social Psychology,* 13, 279–301.

Narcissists Try Harder (or, The Myth That All Good Men Are Taken)

[5]Festinger, L., Schachter S. S., & Back, K. W. (1950). *Social pressures in informal groups.* Starfiord, CA: Starfiord University Press.

[6]Fisher, H. E. (1992). *Anatomy of love: The natural history of monogamy, adultery and divorce.* New York: W.W. Norton.

[7]Rhodewalt, F. & Edding, S. K. (2002). Narcissus reflects: Memory distortion in response to ego relevant feedback in high and low narcissistic men. *Journal of Research in Personality, 36,* 97–116.

Addicted to Drama and Excitement

The Great Satisfaction Drop

[8]Paulhus, D. L. (1998). Interpersonal and intrapsychic adaptiveness of trait self-enhancement: A mixed blessing? *Journal of Personality and Social Psychology, 74,* 1197–1208.

[9]Brunell, A. B., Campbell, W. K., Smith, L., & Krusemark, E. A. (2004, February). *Why do people date narcissists? A narrative study.* Poster presented at the annual meeting of the Society for Personality and Social Psychology, Austin, TX.

[10]Foster, J.D., Shrira, I., & Campbell, W. K. (2003, June). *The trajectory of relationships involving narcissists and non-narcissists.* Poster presented at the annual meeting of the American Psychological Society, Atlanta, GA.

The Double Curse of Dating Narcissists

[11]Festinger, L. (1957). *A Theory of Cognitive Dissonance.* Stanford, CA: Stanford University Press.

[12]Wegner, D. M. (1989). *White bears and other unwanted thoughts: Suppression, obsession, and the psychology of mental control.* New York: Viking/Penguin.

Chapter 4: What Can You Do About it?

Don't Do it—It's a Trap!

[1]Baumeister, R.F., Heatherton, T. F., & Tice, D. M. (1994). *Losing control: How and why people fail at self-regulation*. San Diego, CA: Academic Press.

Have I Done it? Analyzing Your Relationship

[2]Brunell, A. B., Campbell, W. K., Smith, L., & Krusemark, E. A. (2004, February). *Why do people date narcissists? A narrative study*. Poster presented at the annual meeting of the Society for Personality and Social Psychology, Austin, TX.

[3]Foster, J.D., Shrira, I., & Campbell, W. K. (2003, June). *The trajectory of relationships involving narcissists and non-narcissists*. Poster presented at the annual meeting of the American Psychological Society, Atlanta, GA.

Okay, I've Done it—Can Narcissists Change?

[4]Seligman, M. E. P. (1994). What You Can Change and What You Can't. New York: Knopf.

[5]Masterson, J. F. (1988). The search for the real self : Unmasking the personality disorders of our age. Free Press: New York.

[6]Foster, J. D., Campbell, W. K., & Twenge, J. M. (2003). Individual differences in narcissism: Inflated self-views across the lifespan and around the world. *Journal of Research in Personality,* 37, 469–486.

So, Should I Stay or Should I Go?

[7]Rusbult, C. E. & Martz, J. M. (1995). Remaining in an abusive relationship: An investment model analysis of nonvoluntary dependence. *Personality and Social Psychology Bulletin,* 21, 558–571.

Chapter 5: Why Do I Always Date Narcissists?
Is it Society's Fault?

[1]Twenge, J. M., & Campbell, W. K. (2001). Age and birth cohort differences in self-esteem: A cross-temporal meta-analysis. *Personality and Social Psychology Review,* 5, 321–344.

Is it the Narcissist's Fault?

[2]Campbell, W. K., Goodie, A. S., & Foster, J. D. (2004). Narcissism, overconfidence, and risk attitude. *Journal of Behavioral Decision Making*, 17, 297–311.

[3]Robins, R. W., & Beer, J. S. (2001). Positive illusions about the self: Short-term benefits and longterm costs. *Journal of Personality and Social Psychology,* 80, 340–352.

Is it My Fault?

Never Dating a Narcissist Again

Author Bio

W. Keith Campbell is one of the leading authorities on the topic of narcissism and romantic relationships. He has been studying this topic in academic institutions over the last ten years. He completed a doctorate in Social Psychology at the University of North Carolina at Chapel Hill, where his dissertation was titled "Narcissism and Romantic Attraction." Dr. Campbell continued on for two years of postdoctoral training at Case Western Reserve University. Dr. Campbell is currently an Assistant Professor of Psychology at the University of Georgia where he runs a research lab dedicated to understanding the interpersonal lives of narcissists. He also teaches about narcissism in his romantic relationships seminar and social psychology classes.

Dr. Campbell has published a series of scientific and scholarly articles and Chapters on the romantic life of narcissists in some of the nation's premiere psychology journals. He has also been interviewed for numerous newspaper and magazine stories on his research, including stories appearing in the *New York Post*, *USA Today*, *Atlanta Journal-Constitution*, *Shape Magazine*, and *Men's Health*.